DOMER *Dishes*

INSIDE THE LIVES AND KITCHENS OF YOUR FIGHTING IRISH GRIDIRON GREATS!

LISA KELLY

Copy Editor: Kay Clark-Uhles

Cookbook Editors: James Ketara, Kimberly Stevens

Edited & Produced by: Francine Simsky & Rosemary Ellis

Front Cover Photography: Lisa Kelly & James Ketara

Back Cover Photography: Kylie Rose

Portions of some of these stories appeared online as "Where Are They Now" player interviews on NoCoastBias.com, HerLoyalSons.com, and OneFootDown.com under the byline of author Lisa Kelly.

ISBN: 978-1-956464-00-9

The author can be contacted by email at LKND93@sbcglobal.net

DOMER Dishes

INSIDE THE LIVES AND KITCHENS OF YOUR FIGHTING IRISH GRIDIRON GREATS!

LISA KELLY

Lee...

Thank you for having the best idea ever and for letting me run with it.

Karen Phelps Moyer...

Thank you for the inspiration.

Jim...

Thank you for always supporting me and helping me make this cookbook come to life.

Chef James...

Thank you for helping me cook and photograph some of the recipes. I couldn't have done this without you

My Family...

Thank you for helping us eat all of these recipes.

KQ...

Thank you for always being my loudest cheerleader and my rock.

Table of Contents

ALL TEMPERATURES ARE LISTED IN DEGREES FAHRENHEIT

INTRODUCTION

My friends and I were tailgating before the Notre Dame Spring game (the Blue & Gold Game) in 2017 when I was approached with the idea of writing a Notre Dame football cookbook. I had just published my second book the previous fall (*The Men We Became: More Echoes From the End Zone*, which was a follow up to my first book, *Echoes From the End Zone: The Men We Became*) and was looking for my next writing opportunity. I had a few projects in mind, one of which I was seventy pages into, but had kind of stalled on it, when Lee Becton approached me with his idea.

"What do you think about writing a Notre Dame football cookbook that contains the favorite recipes of a bunch of Notre Dame football players, combined with a little storytelling?"

I laughed almost immediately. If you know me, you know I am not a cook. Yes, I cooked for my family as the kids were growing up and managed to not permanently damage anyone, but there are plenty of stories of cooking mishaps that I've been a part of over the years (including burning noodles, which I will never live down). Family rarely allowed me to cook for holiday dinners.

When my parents and grandparents passed the holiday cooking torch to our generation, it didn't get passed to me; it got passed to my husband.

Lee ignored my laughter and told me to think about it. There hadn't been a Notre Dame football cookbook written since the mid-1990s. The gap needed to be filled, and he thought I was just the person to do it. I filed the ask in the back of my brain and decided to move forward on a new project, which was my third book, *Triumphs From Notre Dame: Echoes of Her Loyal Sons & Daughters*.

"I sent out requests for recipes and stories having no idea what the rest of 2020 had in store"

Even as I worked on my third book, every time I ran into Lee, he'd ask, "So have you thought anymore about my idea?" Of course, I had thought about it, and I truly thought it wasn't the right project for me. But after the 2019 football season ended and my book tour wrapped up, I started to seriously consider writing the cookbook.

In January of 2020, I ran the idea by some of my close ND football friends. Everyone's answer was a resounding "Yes! Please, write this cookbook." And so in January of 2020, I started sending out requests for recipes and stories—having no idea what the rest of 2020 would have in store for us. What I thought would be a fun project hit some bumps in the road as we headed into a pandemic in March of 2020, one of which was to deal with some pretty major issues with our family business (a zoo in Branson, Missouri) due to shut downs, significant decreases in tourism, and social unrest that crippled the nation.

After taking some time off to pitch in with the family business, I threw myself back into the recipe-collecting. I figured it would be a positive distraction for all of us, and what could be better than trying out new recipes (with my husband's cooking help, of course)?

"... a positive distraction for all of us, and what could be better than trying out new recipes?"

The road has been winding since I first embarked upon this journey in January of 2020: I've met some new people, rekindled some old friendships, learned A LOT about cooking and photography, and have had a lot of fun trying a wide variety of foods and recipes.

What is Domer Dishes you ask? Well, it's a hybrid of recipes and storytelling. Each ND "chef" in the cookbook has submitted his favorite recipe. Some of them have included a story about why it's their favorite recipe and who or where it came from. Some have shared their most unforgettable Notre Dame memories.

All have shared a little bit of themselves through their best-loved recipes. The cookbook consists of recipes from former Notre Dame football players, coaches, leprechauns, and student managers. And, of course, you'll get one recipe from me. I may not be a very good cook, but there are a couple of things that I do cook well.

This is not a fancy cookbook. I took many of the photos myself as we cooked all the dishes (my husband and I cooked most of them, and my chef friend, James Ketara, helped as well). I hope you enjoy the food and the storytelling that I share in this book. I'd love to know which recipes from the cookbook are your favorite! Please share them with me on Instagram and Twitter by tagging your photos with the hashtag "#DomerDishes."

Well, what are you waiting for? Start cooking!

Cheers! And **GO IRISH**!

Lisa

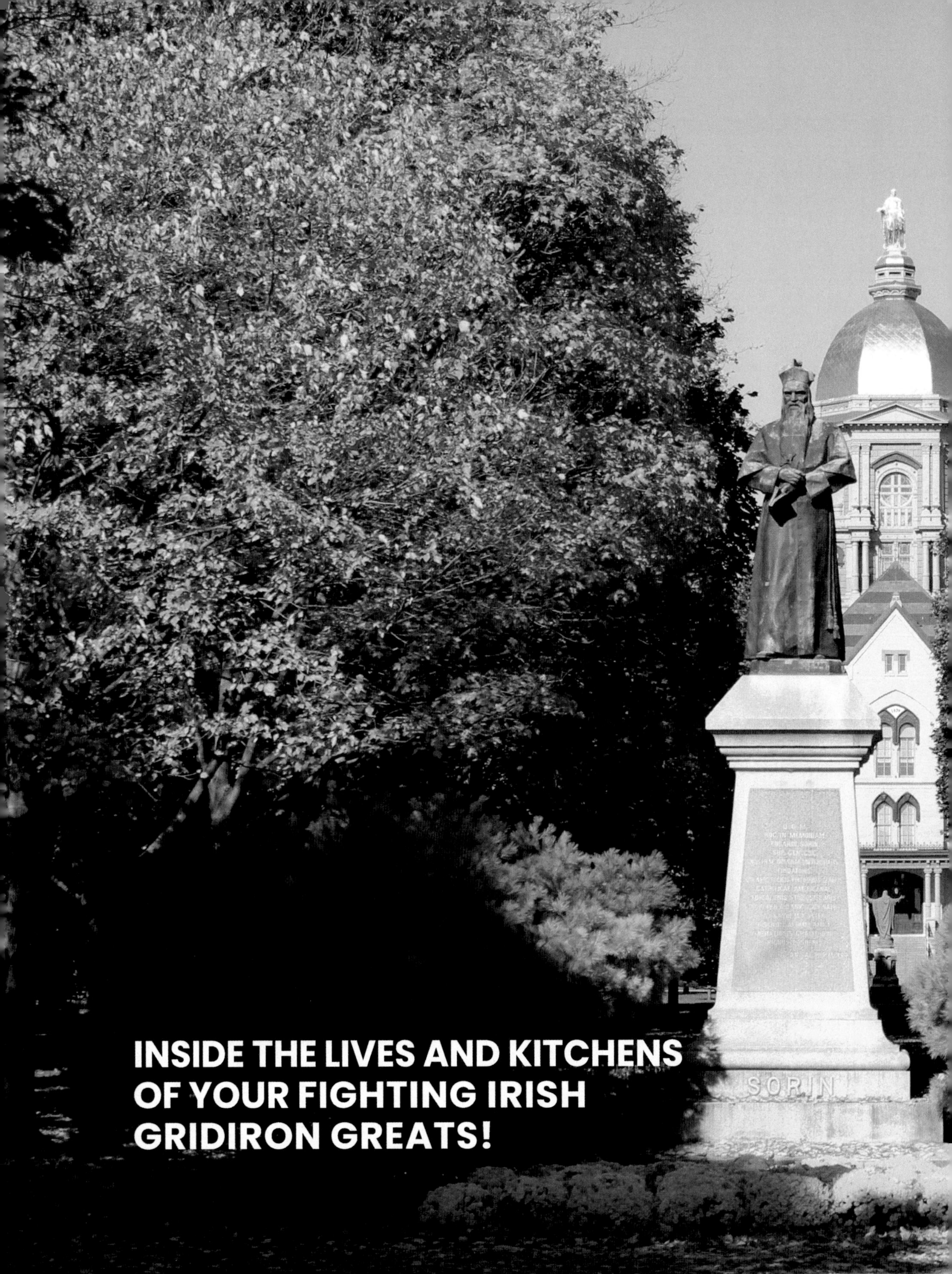
SORIN
INSIDE THE LIVES AND KITCHENS
OF YOUR FIGHTING IRISH
GRIDIRON GREATS!

Braxston Banks

Running Back #39

Braxston Banks (1967–2017) played football at the University of Notre Dame from 1986-1988. He was a wonderful father, son, brother, coach, and mentor to the youth in the Hayward, California community in which he resided. To say that he was a hometown hero would be an understatement. Braxston had a fabled high school career, followed by an outstanding National Championship-winning career at Notre Dame, and later went on to work with and help the young people in his hometown because he wanted to make a difference in their lives. Braxston is greatly missed by all who knew and loved him.

Braxston liked to serve his favorite Sweet Potato Bake with fish (Chilean sea bass, swordfish, or halibut), plus fresh-from-his-garden sliced tomatoes sprinkled with ground pepper and lightly steamed broccoli crowns on the side. His sister, Nicole, so graciously shared this recipe with us all.

Sweet Potato Bake

Ingredients

- 1 40-ounce can or 2 15-ounce cans sweet potatoes
- 5 ounces crushed pineapple
- 5 ounce can evaporated milk (Carnation brand recommended)
- 1 1/2 cups granulated sugar
- 1/2 stick of unsalted butter
- 4 eggs
- 1/2 fresh lemon juice (strain seeds)
- 1/2 teaspoon vanilla extract
- 1/2 teaspoon cinnamon
- 1/2 teaspoon nutmeg

For Pecan Glaze

- 1/3 cup pecans
- 1/2 cup brown sugar
- 1/2 stick unsalted butter

Instructions

For this recipe, you will need a large mixing bowl, a small bowl, a two-quart baking dish, a small pan, and a masher or wooden spoon.

1. Partially unwrap a stick of butter and use the exposed end to grease the sides and bottom of the baking dish.
2. Preheat oven to 350 degrees.
3. In a large mixing bowl, empty the contents of sweet potatoes, first draining and discard the juice, then mash.
   (Alternatively, boil 2 oversized sweet potatoes until fully cooked, peel, and mash.)

Instructions (cont.)

4. In a separate small bowl, beat 4 eggs then add them to the mashed potatoes.
5. Pour small can of evaporated milk into the potato mixture.
6. Add 1 1/2 cups of granulated sugar to mixture in the bowl.
7. Add a small can of crushed pineapple.
8. Add juice from 1/2 of a lemon to the mixture.
9. Add 1/2 teaspoon each of vanilla, cinnamon, and nutmeg.
10. Melt 1/2 stick of butter.
11. Mash ingredients together until smooth using masher or wooden spoon (it is okay if there are a few small lumps of sweet potato).
12. Add melted butter and mix thoroughly.
13. Pour mixture into the greased baking dish and place in the oven to bake for two hours or until a knife inserted comes out clean.
14. While the mixture is baking prepare the Pecan Glaze Topping, which will be poured over the sweet potato mix and baked together.

Pecan Glaze Instructions

1. Melt 1/2 a stick of butter in a small pan.
2. Once melted, remove from heat and stir in 1/4 cup of brown sugar and add 1/2 cup of pecans.
3. Once sweet potatoes are fully cooked remove them from the oven and smooth the pecan mixture over the top.
4. Return to bake in the oven for another 10-15 minutes.
5. Remove the dish and let it cool for 15-20 minutes before serving.

ROCKY BLEIER

HALFBACK #28

ROCKY BLEIER played halfback on the University of Notre Dame football team from 1964-1967. He was selected in the sixteenth round of the 1968 NFL Draft by the Pittsburgh Steelers where he played for one year before he was drafted into the U.S. Army on December 4, 1968.

On August 20, 1969, Rocky was injured in Vietnam. After being told he would never play football again, Rocky spent several years recovering and eventually earned a starting spot on the Steelers' lineup. His illustrious career as a Steeler includes four Steeler Super Bowl victories, 3,865 yards rushing, 136 receptions for 1,294 yards, and 25 touchdowns.

Rocky's favorite recipe is Cauliflower Soup.

Cauliflower Soup

Ingredients

- 1 head of cauliflower, broken into florets
- 1 onion, chopped
- 1 clove garlic, chopped
- 4 cups chicken stock
- olive oil
- salt
- red pepper flakes

Instructions

For this recipe, you will need a large pot and a baking sheet. Preheat oven to 425 degrees.

1. Place florets on baking sheet. Toss with olive oil and salt, add red pepper flakes to taste.
2. Roast at 425-450 for about 15 minutes until browned and tender.
3. Meanwhile, sauté onion in a pot with olive oil (just eyeball how much you need) until soft and lightly browned. When just about done, add garlic for about a minute or so.
4. When cauliflower is done, add to pot with onion and garlic. Add stock and bring to a boil. Turn heat down a bit and continue cooking until cauliflower is very soft and easily pierces with a fork.
5. Let cool a bit and blend in small batches. Adjust for salt.

I sent you a recipe for Cauliflower Soup. First of all, I love soups, all makes and models. With the pandemic in our lives, this past year has been pretty isolating: staying at home, working from home, eating at home with restaurants closed. The eating, snacking, and weight-gaining cycle has been experienced by all. In trying to eat healthy, I came upon this recipe—the great thing is: it's clean! It's only cauliflower with chicken stock. The ingredient that gives it a bite are the red pepper flakes, so don't forget them. Also, I like to make pumpernickel croutons to go along. It goes quickly—I usually make double the recipe. Add the croutons and you are good to go!

—Rocky Bleier

Reggie Brooks

Running Back #40

Ribs by Reggie

Reggie Brooks played running back at the University of Notre Dame from 1989-1993. Reggie played four seasons in the National Football League, predominantly in Washington (1993-95) after the Redskins selected him in the second round of the '93 NFL Draft (45th overall pick). He is currently the executive director of the Holtz's Heroes Foundation. In his role there, he works to carry on the mission of the HHF; that is, helping our former players and teammates by:

1. raising educational scholarships for the children of former players, and
2. efficiently and effectively raising resources and helping manage the Bobby Satterfield Hardship Fund, which is designed to assist former players from Notre Dame under Coach Holtz, or their families, in times of need.

Instructions

My recipe is not really a recipe. It's barbeque. *I grew up in Tulsa, Oklahoma, where barbeque is considered an art form. There's a process to it. It begins and ends with the meat. My preferred slab of rib is pork, particularly* **baby back ribs....**

When choosing a slab or rack of ribs, look for a good ratio of meat to fat (70:30). After your ribs are selected, **season the meat and let it marinate overnight***. I prefer a dry rub, usually sweet and smoky (choose the rub based on your taste or the tastes of your guests).* **Soak your wood chips overnight** *in addition to marinating the meat.*

The wood you choose is incredibly important because it provides the smoky flavor for the ribs. There are a few options out there: hickory, mesquite, apple, cherry, pecan. My preference is apple, with hickory as my other go-to. The day of the BBQ—though others call it "cookout" and "grilling"—I prep the grill or smoker.

I have been a charcoal person my whole life, but recently I've switched to a gas grill (propane). The decision was difficult, but climate change is real and, especially since my middle daughter of five children has encouraged me to be more environmentally conscious, I knew this was the responsible choice. If you are using a charcoal grill/smoker you want to space out your coals as evenly as possible.

Light your coals and let them burn down until they are gray. Once you get them going, **place the wood chips** *that you had soaking overnight over the coals. Again, you want to* **distribute them evenly.** *Place your cleaned grills over hot coals. It's good to have a fairly deep grill bed as this determines the distance the meat is from the fire and the grill time.*

Cook time also depends on the way you cook the meat. Some grills have a smoker away from the fire (this is usually an enclosed compartment attached to the grill) which will take longer, but it will absorb more of the smoke and flavor from the wood chips. **My preferred smoking temperature is between 200 and 250 degrees.** *This usually takes five to seven hours to cook.*

If you grill the ribs, the length of time is shorter but may not be as flavorful or smoky. **My preferred grilling temperature is between 300 and 400 degrees**. *This takes about an hour to an hour and a half to cook.*

With either method, place the ribs bone side down, meat side up. This allows the juices and flavor from the fat to drain down into the meat and the bones. After some cooking time, brush on a little barbeque sauce to lightly coat and cook into the meat. ***At this point, grab a cold beverage of choice, sit back, and let the magic happen.***

—Reggie Brooks

Mike Brown

Leprechaun Mascot

Mike Brown '01 is the Founder and CEO of Soulstir LLC, a social enterprise focused on enriching lives by creating experiences that inspire empowerment and action, and a Regional Director for Athletics Advancement in University Relations at the University of Notre Dame. As a Notre Dame student, he served two years as the iconic Notre Dame Leprechaun mascot and was the first Black student to portray the role. He is a former Director on the ND Alumni Association and Monogram Club boards, and serves as a leader on diversity, equity, and inclusion initiatives. When not watching or attending ND sporting events he enjoys writing and running. Originally from Milwaukee, he now lives in the South Bend area with his wife, Jaymie '02,'03, and daughter, Harper.

Chicken, Cheese, & Rice

Ingredients

- 1 large box Minute Rice
- 2 packages mild cheddar cheese
- 2 cans cream of chicken soup
- 2 packages of Purdue Shortcuts carved chicken breast
- 2 tablespoons garlic powder
- 1 teaspoon black pepper

Instructions

For this recipe, you will need a saucepan, a large pot, and a 9"x13"x2" deep baking dish.

1. Bring 4 1/3 cups of water to a boil in saucepan.
2. Add 4 cups of rice, then tightly cover for 10 minutes.
3. Put 2 cans of cream of chicken soup in a pot with 2 cans of water. Warm and stir until smooth.
4. After rice is done, spread half of rice throughout the baking dish.
5. Spread 1 pack of carved chicken breast chunks over rice (if chunks are large, break apart).
6. Pour half of soup over chicken and rice.
7. Sprinkle 1 package of shredded cheese over the layers so far, followed by a sprinkle of garlic poweder and pepper.
8. Spread remaining rice over cheese layer.
9. Preheat oven to 350 degrees and repeat steps 5–7, ending with cheese and seasonings on top.
10. Place dish with chicken, cheese, and rice in oven for approximately 30 minutes.
11. Remove from oven, let stand for 5 minutes, and serve.

I didn't know my dad was a good cook until around 2008 when my wife and I stopped by his house for a Thanksgiving meal. The meal was so good we had to take to-go plates because we loved his cooking—especially his chicken, cheese, and rice—so much. I was raised by my mom's side of my family. My dad and I had a cordial relationship that was fine on the surface.

If you go beyond the surface though, unbeknownst to him, for nearly thirty-five years, I carried a pain within my heart because he was not engaged in my life. I summoned the courage to share the pain I felt with him in June of 2019, and we've been on a beautiful journey of healing ever since. Sharing his recipe as my contribution to this book is a big deal for me personally, and I do so with great pride and joy. Thank you, and I love you, Charles Walton.

—Mike Brown

Te'Von Coney

Linebacker #4

Te'Von Coney played football at the University of Notre Dame from 2015-2018. He went undrafted in the 2019 NFL Draft and has been on the off-season and/or practice squad for the Oakland/Las Vegas Raiders for two seasons (2019-2020). Te'von currently runs his foundation, Tough Choices, which serves to educate, inspire, and mentor youth from communities in dire need of additional, equitable support.

We maintain that it is essential to be able to connect and build with the youth on platforms with components they can identify with. Tough Choices is not a brand, but a movement crafted to encourage change, reform education, and spark growth.

Te'von also works on the Onóra TC Whiskey team and his favorite recipe is hot wings.

Hot Wings

Ingredients

- Dash salt-free Original Seasoning Blend
- Badia Complete Seasoning
- Lawry's Seasoned Salt
- Crisco Vegetable Oil
- Sweet Baby Ray's Buffalo sauce

Instructions

For this recipe, you will need two mixing bowls and a Dutch oven or similar dish alternative.

1. In a Dutch oven, add the Crisco oil and heat to 360 degrees, monitoring frequently.
2. In a medium mixing bowl, add Lawry's seasoned salt, Badia, and Dash (salt free), and whisk until well combined.
3. Lay wings out on a sheet tray, and with a paper towel, pat dry.
4. Add wings to the mixing bowl of seasonings and toss to coat.
5. With oil temperature at 360, add wings one at a time and fry until done.
6. While wings are frying, add the Buffalo Sauce to a mixing bowl. Set aside.
7. Remove wings when finished, and add immediately to the bowl of buffalo sauce, toss, and plate.

Chef James Notes: *It is always best to dry off poultry that is going to be fried. Poultry holds water, which is a bad combination for frying preparations.*

Growing up I was a really picky eater and didn't have much variety in what I ate. Most times, I would eat at different fast-food restaurants and get chicken nuggets. Outside of that, I basically only ate pizza and breakfast foods—that was my diet for many years. Still to this day, I haven't found a way to expand what I like, so I eat the same things. Growing up, I was never in the kitchen when my parents cooked, but one day my mom brought me into the kitchen and said, "Instead of going to all these different restaurants and spending all your money on chicken wings, I'm going to teach you how to make your own hot wings." Now, I have this meal about two times a week; this wings recipe became my favorite and changed my life.

While studying at the University of Notre Dame, I was taught how to use my talents to be a powerful force of good. I developed disciplined habits of mind, body, and spirit to accomplish the many goals I had set for my life. Onóra Whiskey is a reflection of my commitment to honor and respect the common good. In Irish Gaelic, Onóra stands for "honor" and is a diverse group of unique, determined, and dedicated individuals brought together by an idea and held together by values. Onóra Whiskey holds true to the belief that everyone should be respected equally and be given the same opportunities to lead a successful life. We respect all and we care. We know that together we can change the world for the better. We hope you enjoy our hard work and that you help change the world with us.

—Te'Von Coney

Lake Dawson

Wide Receiver #87

Lake Dawson played wide receiver at the University of Notre Dame from 1990-1994. He was drafted by the Kansas City Chiefs in the 1994 NFL Draft where he played for four years, followed by two years with the Indianapolis Colts. After he retired from playing football, he transitioned into working on the business side of the NFL, working in his hometown of Seattle for the Seattle Seahawks from 2001-2007, the Tennessee Titans from 2007-2015, and the Cleveland Browns from 2015-17. He is currently the assistant director of college scouting for the Buffalo Bills. Lake's favorite recipe is his mom's Sweet Potato Pie.

Photo by Marlene "Ma" Dawson

Ma's Sweet Potato Pie

Ingredients

- 1 pre-made 8-inch pie crust
- 1 1/4 cups sweet potatoes, mashed
- 1 1/2 cups sugar, white
- 2 eggs, beaten
- 1/4 teaspoon nutmeg
- 1/2 teaspoon cinnamon
- 1/2 teaspoon salt
- 1 teaspoon pure vanilla extract
- 1 cup sweetened condensed milk
- 1 stick of butter, melted

Instructions

For this recipe, you will need an 8-inch pie crust. Preheat oven to 425 degrees.

1. Beat cooked sweet potatoes until smooth.
2. Add sugar, eggs, vanilla extract, spices, and salt. Blend thoroughly.
3. Add milk and melted butter, stir.
4. Pour into pie crust pan.
5. Bake at 425 degrees for 20 minutes.
6. Reduce temperature to 300 degrees and bake 50 minutes longer.

Simply put, this recipe reminds me of all the love and support I received from home. I love both my parents and appreciate the discipline my dad taught me, but the feelings I have toward my mom or "Ma", as I called her, are special. She is the beat of my heart and taught me through her work ethic and love. I recall her sending me sweet potato pies in the mail my freshman year at Notre Dame, to encourage me and help me not feel homesick. I also remember her making pies for my entire team when I played professional football for the Kansas City Chiefs. Whenever we played in my hometown against the Seattle Seahawks, she made sure to have several pies waiting near our buses after the game. My Chiefs teammates always looked forward to her pies each year we played Seattle. Everything my mother does she does with love, energy, and a strong work ethic. I can't imagine how long it took her to make pies for a NFL roster of fifty-three-plus men, but she did it every time. Ma's sweet potato pie will always be my favorite dessert recipe! Go Irish!

—Lake Dawson

AUTRY DENSON

RUNNING BACK #23

AUTRY DENSON played football at the University of Notre Dame from 1995-1998 and played four years professionally in the National Football League for the Miami Dolphins, the Indianapolis Colts, and the Chicago Bears. After spending some time away from the game, Autry returned to football as a coach and currently serves as the head coach of the Charleston Southern Buccaneers in the Big South Conference.

Autry's recipe, Blossom's Oxtails with rice and peas, is submitted on behalf of his brother and friend, Marlon R. Llewellyn (Carol "Blossom" Campbell's son).

Blossom's Jamaican Oxtails with Rice & Peas

Ingredients

- 2–3 pounds beef oxtails, trimmed
- 2 cups water
- ½ bell pepper
- ½ scotch bonnet pepper (or habanero)
- 1 yellow onion
- 3 sprigs fresh thyme
- 1 green onion
- 2 tablespoons fresh garlic
- 3 tablespoons browning sauce
- 2 tablespoons black pepper
- 2 tablespoons garlic powder
- 2 tablespoons seasoned salt
- 2 tablespoons allspice
- 2 tablespoons kosher salt
- 2 tablespoons corn starch

Instructions

For this recipe, you will need a crockpot or Instant pot, a large baking sheet, and a saucepan. Preheat oven to 500 degrees (broil).

1. Chop all vegetables (peppers, onions, and garlic). Set aside for Step 4.
2. Season and coat oxtails evenly with browning sauce, 1 tbsp black pepper, seasoned salt, allspice, garlic powder, and kosher salt.
3. Place seasoned oxtails on baking sheet, place on bottom rack of broiled oven, and brown each side for 7 to 10 minutes, ensuring each side is browned evenly.
4. Remove browned oxtails from oven and transfer to crock or instant pot and add vegetables, remaining black pepper, thyme, and water.
5. For crock pot, set to high for 1 hour. For instant pot, use the meat/stew setting for 20 minutes (refer to manual for specifics). Remove oxtails from pot when done.
6. In a saucepan, add two cups of liquid from the pot and the cornstarch. Whisk until smooth, heat to reduce by half, and taste for seasoning.
7. Serve oxtails with rice and peas (recipe to follow), pour gravy over the oxtails, and enjoy!

Rice & Peas

Ingredients

- 2 cups rice
- ½ cup coconut milk
- 1 can red kidney beans, drained
- ½ stick of butter (¼ cup)
- 2 sprigs fresh thyme
- 1 green onion
- 2 tablespoons salt
- 1 tablespoon sugar
- 2 tablespoons black pepper
- 1 tablespoon garlic powder
- 1 tablespoon seasoned salt

Instructions

For this recipe, you will need a rice cooker or pot

1. Add ingredients and 3 cups water to rice cooker and sit back or follow instructions for rice.
2. Serve with oxtail and enjoy!

This recipe is inspired by the sacred Caribbean trade winds of an island rooted in faith, love, sun, and reggae music. It honors a woman who was like another mother to me, Mrs. Carol Beverley Campbell, affectionately known as "Blossom." Blossom and her family migrated to the United States in the early 1970s from a small rural town in Clarendon, Jamaica, where her father, Curtis, was a sharecropper on a sugarcane plantation; her mother, Gwendolyn, cared for the small family home, which included three girls and four boys.

Blossom was the second born and the protector of her siblings. From Blossom's humble beginnings, starting in rural Jamaica, the family moved to Fort Lauderdale, Florida. There, I was fortunate and blessed to witness her magic as she instilled in me the importance of faith, family, loyalty, respect, fun, and love for Jamaican cuisine and family gatherings. Family came first. Even though I was not her biological son, you wouldn't know the difference. I had an open invitation to enter the home any time, play video games with my brothers, and enjoy a meal prepared with love.

Blossom wore many hats. Mother, daughter, wife, sister, aunt, friend, nurse, seamstress, caterer, and fabulous cook. But most importantly, she was a believer. She believed in Jesus Christ and understood that her faith could and would move mountains.

Sadly, Blossom transitioned to be with our Lord on May 14, 2014, after a long-fought battle with mental illness and dementia complications at fifty-nine years of age. Her contagious smile and delectable food are greatly missed. She is the reason I am sharing with you Blossom's almost-famous Jamaican Oxtails with Rice and Peas recipe. It epitomizes the woman I grew to love and who inspired me like my very own mother. My prayer is that you and your family will be as blessed by this dish as my family and me. It is also my wish that you be inspired by this brief glimpse of a woman, who left a blossoming legacy through her love, faith, family, and food.

—Autry Denson

Tony Driver

Defensive Back #25

Tony Driver played football at the University of Notre Dame from 1997-2000. He was drafted in the sixth round of the 2001 NFL Draft by the Buffalo Bills, where he played for two seasons. Tony and his family currently live in Louisville, Kentucky. Tony's favorite recipe is his mom's Broccoli Casserole.

My mom made this dish every Thanksgiving and Christmas, and I started to help her when I was five years old. Over the years, I've kept tweaking the recipe. I hope you enjoy it as much as I do!

—Tony Driver

Broccoli Casserole

Ingredients

- 2 heads of broccoli
- 1 stick of butter
- 2 10.75-ounce cans cream of mushroom soup
- 16 ounces Velveeta cheese
- 2 sleeves Ritz crackers (approximately)
- 1 ½ teaspoons of Salt
- 2 teaspoons of pepper

Instructions

For this recipe, you will need an approximately 9″x13″ casserole dish and two pots.

1. Rinse and cut the broccoli leaving about 2-3 inches of the stem on the buds.
2. Use butter to grease casserole dish and boil water in one pot.
3. Add the broccoli, remaining butter, salt, and pepper to boiling water.
4. Boil broccoli until tender. You should be able to slice through it with a fork.
5. Strain the water out thoroughly and preheat oven to 350 degrees.
6. In second pot, boil the mushroom soup, adding enough water so it is flexible enough to pour (~1 cup of water).
7. Thinly slice the Velveeta cheese to layer in the casserole.

Instructions (cont.)

8. Layer the ingredients:
    - 1st layer: Evenly spread the broccoli on the bottom of the pan.
    - 2nd layer: Crush the crackers evenly over the broccoli.
    - 3rd layer: Lightly layer the cheese slices over the crackers about 2 inches apart. (remember to save some for the other layers)
    - 4th layer: Spread the mushroom soup over the cheese slices.
9. Repeat layers until you reach the top of your baking dish. The top layer should be finished with crushed crackers.
10. Bake 45–60 minutes at 350 degrees. The ingredients should mesh, and the top layer of crackers will start to brown.
11. Remove from oven, let cool, serve, and enjoy!

Marc Edwards

Fullback #44

Marc Edwards played football at the University of Notre Dame from 1993-1997. His NFL career consisted of playing for five NFL teams, including the San Francisco 49ers, Cleveland Browns, New England Patriots, Jacksonville Jaguars, and Chicago Bears. During his time with the Patriots (2001 season), he helped to win the 2002 Super Bowl. Marc's favorite recipe is his Baby Back Ribs.

Baby Back Ribs

Ingredients

- Slab of baby back ribs
- Montreal Steak Seasoning
- Preferred BBQ sauce

Instructions

For this recipe, you will need a large roasting pan and a grill. Preheat oven to 250 degrees.

1. Cut baby back rib slab into quarters.
2. Season both sides of each quarter with Montreal Steak Seasoning.
3. Use non-stick spray on aluminum foil and double wrap each quarter of seasoned ribs.
4. Place in roasting pan and bake at 250 degrees for 3 hours.
5. Remove from foil when done, then coat both sides of the ribs with your preferred BBQ sauce.
6. Spray grill with non-stick spray.
7. Sear ribs on grill for 5 to 10 minutes on each side to your preference.
8. Enjoy as these ribs literally fall off the bone!

Marc Edwards's Notre Dame Highlight:

Marc's time at Notre Dame was full of successes under Head Coach Lou Holtz. He experienced a huge high in his collegiate career during the Notre Dame–USC game his junior year (1995) when Notre Dame was an underdog headed into the match up.

Photo by Marc Edwards

At that point, we had beaten USC for ten straight years. In the eleventh year, we tied them, and here we were the underdogs of this meeting. It was Keyshawn Johnson's senior year. USC was undefeated going into the game, and we were coming in 5–2. It was being hyped as the year that USC was going to come into our house and beat us. And what happened? We came out and put a major beating on them. Physically, mentally, we beat them in all aspects of the game. I probably had the best game of my life. I ran like crazy that game, scored three touchdowns, threw for a two-point pass, ran for a two-point conversion, and ended up being carried off the field. I was the NBC Player of the Game. It was a surreal experience. We beat USC 38-10. It was the first time I was an integral part of a big-time victory as a starter.

—Marc Edwards

Pat Eilers

Safety #13

Pat Eilers played both football and baseball at the University of Notre Dame and was a member of the 1988 National Championship football squad. He graduated with a biology (pre-med) degree in 1989 and a mechanical engineering degree in 1990. Pat went on to play football in the NFL for the Minnesota Vikings, Washington Redskins, and Chicago Bears before embarking upon a successful career in the private equity industry. Pat currently lives in Chicago with his wife. They have four children. Pat's favorite recipe is Chicken Gyros and Homemade Hummus with Whipped Feta.

Chicken Gyros & Hummus with Whipped Feta

Ingredients

- 2 pounds boneless, skinless chicken breast
- 4 tablespoons extra virgin olive oil
- 6 garlic cloves, minced
- 2 tablespoons oregano
- 4 teaspoons salt
- 2 teaspoons pepper
- 1 cup water
- ½ cup lemon juice
- 6 tablespoons red wine vinegar

Toppings, As desired

Cucumbers, diced
Peppers, diced
Tomatoes, diced
Whipped feta
Hummus
Mixed greens

Gyro Instructions

For this recipe, you will need a Dutch oven or a similar dish alternative. Preheat oven to 400 degrees. Following, you will need a food processor.

1. Add all ingredients into the Dutch oven and bake for 1 ½ hours.
2. Shred chicken in the Dutch oven using two forks (this is what I do!) and let them sit in the juice for another 15 minutes before serving.
3. Recommended: serve as an open plate with pita, tzatziki sauce, and toppings.

(See following page for hummus and whipped feta recipes)

Hummus & Whipped Feta

Hummus Ingredients

- 2 cups canned chickpeas, drained, liquid reserved
- 1 1/2 teaspoons kosher salt
- 4 garlic cloves, minced
- 1/3 cup tahini (sesame paste)
- 6 tablespoons freshly squeezed lemon juice
- 2 lemons
- 2 tablespoons water or liquid from the chickpeas
- 8 dashes Tabasco sauce

Whipped Feta Ingredients

- 6 ounces of good feta, crumbled
- 6 ounces cream cheese, room temp
- 1/3 cup extra virgin olive oil
- 2 tablespoons lemon juice
- 1/2 teaspoon kosher salt
- 1/2 teaspoon pepper

Hummus Instructions

Place all the ingredients in the bowl of a food processor fitted with a steel blade and process until the hummus is coarsely puréed. Taste for seasoning and serve chilled or at room temperature.

Whipped Feta Instructions

Place feta and cream cheese in the food processor, blend until smooth. Add the olive oil while the machine is running, then the lemon juice, salt, and pepper.

Photos by Pat & Jana Eilers

Pat Eilers's Notre Dame Highlight:

During the 1988 Notre Dame–Miami game, Miami's quarterback, Steve Walsh, had also been the quarterback of my high school rival, Cretin. In my senior year of high school, we beat Cretin during the regular season when I intercepted Steve twice, but they went on to beat us in the first playoff game. (Walsh and I also played together when we were both with the Chicago Bears.) Now, we were playing against each other on a much bigger stage.

A lot of people from St. Paul came to see both of us play. Steve played really well that day, but thankfully we won. Coach Holtz called my number when we were close to the Miami goal line. I scored the first touchdown of my career. It was a thrill to look up and see the mural on the library building over the top of the north end of the stadium, "Touchdown Jesus." Beating Miami is something I will never forget. They came into the game ranked number one and hadn't lost in a couple of years. Our 1988 Notre Dame team went on to an undefeated season and won the national championship. Truly an unforgettable year.

—Pat Eilers

Mike Elston

Defensive Line Coach

Mike Elston has been a football coach at the University of Notre Dame since 2010. He played football at the University of Michigan and, prior to coaching at Notre Dame, coached at Michigan, Central Michigan, and Cincinnati. Mike's favorite recipe is his Notre Dame Defensive Line Ribs.

For this recipe, you will need a large, heavy-duty steam table pan (3 to 4 racks should fit into one) and some tinfoil.

Defensive Line Ribs

The Preparation

1. First, unpackage the ribs (duh) then peel the white membrane off the back of the ribs with a damp paper towel. (I prefer this because I want the meat to fall off the bone, if you like a little snap on the rib, leave the membrane on, yuck.)
2. Next, thoroughly rinse the ribs and dry with a paper towel.
3. Generously cover every square inch of the ribs with your favorite dry rub. I do not make my own. (I prefer something a little smoky & sweet.)
4. Place the ribs in the steam table pan and cover with normal tinfoil.
5. Refrigerate overnight and until you are 4 to 5 hours from serving your guests.

The Main Event

1. Take the ribs out and allow to rest at room temperature for about an hour (not much longer).
2. Preheat your grill to 500 degrees and preheat your oven to 300 degrees.
3. When grill is up to temp, toss your ribs on the grill for 15 minutes on each side. Do not leave the grill. You do not want the ribs to catch fire. Trust me on that one!
4. Once ribs have a nice char or bark, remove from grill & replace into pan. Cover thoroughly with tinfoil.
5. Once covered, place in 300 degree oven for 2 hours. (Cook time will be long if you have 6 or more racks of ribs.)
6. Once ribs are done (you'll know because the house will smell amazing), remove ribs from oven and let sit for 15 to 20 minutes.
7. Serving methods:
    a) You can serve them dry rubbed with a side of sauce.
    b) You can quarter them with a knife or serve them full racks.
    c) My preferred method: cut them three to four ribs at a time & smother with my favorite BBQ sauce!
    (A Cincinnati Favorite: Montgomery Inn BBQ sauce, found at Kroger.)

This recipe is my go-to when I have my players at the house for bonding and fellowship. The preparation is easy and the finishing steps do not have you harnessed to a grill, so you can move around and entertain. Before preparing this recipe, I must warn you that you'll need to sign a waiver because these ribs are so tender and so delicious people have been known to eat their fingers! I cannot be liable for that and that's where the waiver comes in. When grilling anything, the quality of the meat is key. I have a tendency to purchase prime meat, including the best quality pork ribs I can find. The place that I have had the most success with great quality meat is Costco. I'll buy anywhere from three to six racks of ribs at a time, based on how many people I'm entertaining. I prefer baby-back ribs or pork ribs and don't mess with the others. Remember, preparation is key and the recipe starts twenty-four hours before the fun begins! Enjoy and GO IRISH!

—Mike Elston

Tony Fisher

Running Back #12

Tony Fisher, class of 2002, played running back at the University of Notre Dame. In 1997, Fisher won the prestigious "Mr. Football" award as the best football player in the state of Ohio. After graduating from Notre Dame, he was signed as a free agent by the Green Bay Packers where he played from 2002–2005, followed by a year with the St. Louis Rams (2006). In 2013, the Packers hired him as their player/alumni senior coordinator. The Euclid High School football grad also has an award named after him (the Fisher Award). He makes an effort to meet the winner of the award every year, even during the 2020 pandemic. Tony's favorite recipe is his mom's Banana Pudding (which you can also find on the Nilla Wafer box).

Banana Pudding

Ingredients

- 3/4 cup sugar, divided
- 1/3 Cup all-purpose flour
- pinch of salt
- 3 eggs, yolks separated
- 2 cups milk
- 1/2 teaspoon vanilla extract
- 45 vanilla wafers, divided
- 5 Medium ripe bananas (about 3 1/2 cups, sliced)

Instructions

For this recipe, you will need a baking dish and a double boiler (two pots). This recipe serves 6–8 with a prep time of 10 minutes and cook time of 30 minutes.

1. Preheat oven to 350 degrees.
2. Mix 1/3 cup sugar, flour, and salt in a double boiler. Add 3 egg yolks and milk. Cook uncovered, over boiling water 10-12 minutes, stirring constantly. Remove from heat; stir in vanilla extract.
3. Reserve 12 vanilla wafers for garnish.
4. Spread small amount of custard on bottom of baking dish; cover with layers: 1/3 each of the remaining wafers, sliced bananas, then custard over bananas.
5. Continue to layer wafers, bananas, and custard to make a total of 3 layers each, ending with custard.
6. Beat egg whites on high speed until soft peaks form.

Instructions (cont.)

7. Gradually, add remaining ¼ cup sugar, beating until stiff peaks form.
8. Spread mixture evenly over top layer of custard to cover; sealing well to edge.
9. Bake 15–20 minutes, until browned.
10. Cool slightly. Insert the 12 remaining wafers along inside edge of cooked pudding.
11. Serve and don't forget to share!

This is my favorite banana pudding that my mom has been making for years!

—Tony Fisher

Reggie Fleurima

Defensive Tackle #94

Reggie Fleurima, former defensive tackle, played football for the University of Notre Dame from 1991-1994. Reggie currently lives with his family in the Chicago suburbs. You can catch him on his sports podcast, the ***Big Flo Show***, on Facebook and YouTube or ***The Ball Hog Sports Talk*** with fellow Irish football alum Bobby Brown on Facebook and all major podcast platforms.

Big Flo's Chicken Wings

Ingredients

Buttermilk Brine & Seasonings

- 1 quart buttermilk
- 4 teaspoons kosher salt
- 1 teaspoon freshly ground black pepper
- Tony Chachere's Creole Seasoning (to taste)

Baste Preparation & Seasonings

- Walkerswood jerk seasoning
- 2 parts Worcestershire sauce
- 1 part beer
- 1 part apple cider vinegar
- Montreal Steak Seasoning (to taste)

Instructions

For this recipe, you will need a large, resealable plastic bag and use a smoker and/or grill. This recipe is for 3½–4 pounds of wings.

1. Combine chicken wings, buttermilk, kosher salt, and black pepper in the resealable plastic bag. Chill at least 4 hours or overnight.
2. After chilling, drain brine and rinse.
3. Season with Tony Chachere's Creole Seasoning.
4. Split the chicken into two batches. Add a jar of Walkerswood mild jerk seasoning (or spicy, if you want to step up the heat!) to one half of the wings, leave the other half without.
5. Let wings sit at room temp for 1 hour. Meanwhile, prep grill or smoker.
6. Cook on a smoker at 250 degrees or indirect heat on your grill until your wings' probe temperature is 170 degrees.
7. Baste wings every 20–30 minutes. With smoker method, if skin is not crispy enough, transfer to a hot grill for 5 minutes, flipping constantly.
8. Serve wings, decide which batch you like the best, and enjoy!

I created this wing recipe by piecing together techniques from fellow grill masters. Thank you KJ and DC! But it is my unique combination that makes these wings the hit at every tailgate. The brine makes them juicy. The seasoning makes them flavorful. The baste adds the extra zing. Warning: Once you make them this way, your friends and family won't accept them any other way!

—Reggie Fleurima

John Foley

Linebacker #49

John Foley was a linebacker at the University of Notre Dame from 1986-1987. Even though John's football career at Notre Dame was short, he made the absolute best of his time there.

When John started his career and family, he traveled frequently for work. His son, Ryan, figured he would step up and cook to help his mom. Today, his son is an amazing cook.

I did not miss my kids' sports, but I did miss many dinners. Here is John's favorite recipe, his son's Smoked BBQ Beef Ribs.

When asked what his best football memory at Notre Dame was, it was an off-the-field experience that first came to his mind.

Smoked BBQ Beef Ribs

Ingredients

- 3–4 pounds beef ribs
- 3 tablespoons beer rub
- 3 tablespoons mustard
- Stubs Original BBQ Sauce
- moistening spray, in bottle (equal parts apple juice and apple cider vinegar)

Instructions

For this recipe,you will use a smoker and need a food-safe spray bottle.

1. Preheat smoker to 250 degrees.
2. Remove silver skin (membrane) from ribs.
3. Apply thin layer of mustard to ribs as a binding agent.
4. Apply beer rub on meat and bone side.
5. Place ribs on smoker, meat side up.
6. Cook 3–4 hours, spraying every hour to keep from drying out.
7. Raise temperature to 375 degrees for 30 minutes.
8. Sauce ribs 5 minutes before done, in smoker.
9. Serve and enjoy!

Photos by John Foley

Author's Note: This recipe pairs nicely with a glass of Cabernet Sauvignon, from Notre Dame alumni Rick Mirer's ***Mirror Napa Valley*** *(see page 114).*

John Foley's Notre Dame Highlight:

Absolutely, positively for me it was the national title game. Surreal! I was supposed to start as the Sporting News preseason All-American, but I didn't even get to play in the game. Because of the work I had done with the coaching staff, though, I was on the field. The guys treated me like I was part of the team, and I really thank them for that. That's also how I got my national title ring. The National Championship game was special. It's amazing how close the Notre Dame family bond is. It's an instant connection. Today, when I do work on Wall Street, I work with a lot of Notre Dame graduates. They trust me because we have that bond.

Tony Furjanic

Linebacker #53

Tony Furjanic was a linebacker on the University of Notre Dame football team and co-captain during the 1985 season. In the 1986 NFL Draft, Tony was drafted by the Buffalo Bills where he played from 1986-1987. He then played one year with the Miami Dolphins in 1988. Tony currently works in medical sales at Forthright, Inc., in the Cape Coral, Florida area. Tony's favorite recipe is his mom's Linguini with Clam Sauce, followed by her Chocolate Chip Cookies.

Linguini with Clam Sauce & Chocolate Chip Cookies

Ingredients

Linguini

- 1 pound linguini
- 1/4 cup olive oil
- 1 stick butter
- 5 cloves garlic, crushed
- 1 1/4 cups water
- 3/4 cup dry vermouth
- 2 8-ounce bottles clam juice
- 1 teaspoon salt
- 1 teaspoon oregano (approximately)
- 2 cans clam sauce
- Romano cheese, to taste
- black pepper, to taste
- parsley, to taste

Cookies

- 1 pound margarine (3 sticks butter + 1 stick margarine)
- 2 cups brown sugar, packed
- 2 egg yolks
- 4 cups flour
- 1 12-ounce package chocolate chips
- 1 cup nuts, chopped (optional)
- 1/4 teaspoon salt
- 1–2 teaspoons vanilla

These are my favorite recipes. My mom would make the linguini (or some form of pasta) for me before every game in high school. The chocolate chip cookies recipe has been in our family for over thirty-five years—it's a favorite with all!

Linguini with Clam Sauce

Instructions

1. Cook linguini to box instructions and drain.
2. Mix together all ingredients for sauce except linguini and clams, heat.
3. Add clams over linguini and toss to mix.
4. Pour heated sauce over pasta and add grated Romano cheese and parsley.
5. Add pepper and more cheese to taste.

Instructions

1. Preheat oven to 350 degrees.
2. Cream margarine and brown sugar.
3. Add egg yolks and blend well.
4. Thoroughly mix in flour, 1 cup at a time.
5. Add salt, vanilla, chocolate chips, and chopped nuts.
6. Using a teaspoon, drop walnut-sized dough onto ungreased baking sheet.
7. Bake 10-12 minutes, let cool, and enjoy!

Ty Goode

Cornerback #24

Ty Goode played cornerback at the University of Notre Dame from 1994-1997. He currently resides in his hometown of Lincoln, Nebraska, and is a supervisor at Nelnet, a technology and services company, which provides payment technology for education loans. Nelnet delivers world-class fiber Internet, TV, and phone services to residents of Nebraska and Colorado, helps borrowers achieve their educational goals with private student loans and refinance solutions, and helps businesses boost their performance with cutting-edge technology and trusted expertise.

Ty's favorite recipe is a New York Style Creamy Cheesecake.

New York Style Creamy Cheesecake

Ingredients

Crust

- 16–18 graham crackers
- 1/4 cup almonds
- 1/4 cup sugar
- 1 stick butter, melted (can substitute margarine)

Filling

MUST BE AT ROOM TEMPERATURE

- 36 ounces cream cheese
- 5 eggs
- 3/4 cup sour cream
- 1 tablespoon vanilla
- 1 tablespoon lemon juice
- 1/4 cup flour
- 1 3/4 cup sugar
- 1/2 teaspoon salt

I learned as a college student cooking from scratch is normally cheaper and tastier than going out to eat. My favorite dessert has always been cheesecake. But to get the "good ones," it gets pretty hard on the wallet. So I started testing different cheesecake recipes as a result of a dare from a coworker who is a phenomenal baker. After a couple years of experimentation, I settled on this New York Style Creamy Cheesecake recipe. Why? Because it will allow you to add any flavor you want to it for your taste buds. But you don't have to! To me, it's that good. My cheesecakes have been requested for Mother's Day, Father's Day, and birthdays. I hope you enjoy it as much as I do.

—Ty Goode

For this recipe, you will need a 10 inch springform pan, food processor or blender, stand mixer or hand mixer, baking sheet, spatula, and a rounded drinking glass.

Instructions

1. Preheat oven to 350 degrees.
2. For crust, blend almonds, crackers, and sugar until the texture is like coarse sand, then, one half at a time, add melted butter and pulse until incorporated.
3. Pour crust mixture into springform to coat the bottom. Use the bottom of round glass and evenly spread and flatten mixture from the center to edge. (Alternatively, you can use your hands to press crust into place.)
4. Place the springform onto sheet and bake on middle rack for 8 to 10 minutes. When done, set aside to cool.
5. Add cream cheese to stand mixer 8 ounces at a time, scraping down sides of bowl to ensure everything is smooth.
6. Add the sugar, salt, lemon juice, and vanilla. Thoroughly mix until smooth. Then, add sour cream and mix until combined and smooth.
7. STOP!!! At this point, taste the mixture and make any additions if needed, then proceed.
8. Add one egg at a time, mixing to blend thoroughly between each egg. Then add flour and mix until thoroughly combined and smooth.
9. Once crust is cool to the touch, ensure springform is still on baking sheet and pour filling into the pan.
10. Bake at 350 degrees for 10 minutes. Then, reduce to 300 degrees and bake for an additional 40–50 minutes.
11. Remove from oven and let cool to room temperature. Once cooled, set in refrigerator for 2 to 3 hours.
12. When time to serve, remove from springform, add your favorite toppings or decoration, and enjoy!

Bill Hackett

Kicker #18

Bill Hackett played football for the University of Notre Dame from 1988-1991 and played on the 1988 National Championship team. Bill's favorite recipe is his mom's Steamed Chocolate Pudding.

*The **Barbara Sylvia Hackett's Steamed Chocolate Pudding** is steeped in tradition just like Notre Dame. The recipe will test your patience, but the end result will melt in your mouth and keep you coming back for more. The pudding is very filling and requires a walk with your family after you have enjoyed it. From my family to yours. Go Irish!*

—Bill Hackett

Barbara Sylvia Hackett's Steamed Chocolate Pudding

Ingredients

For Pudding

- 3 tablespoons shortening
- 2/3 cup sugar
- 1 egg, well beaten
- 3 teaspoons baking powder
- 2 1/2 cups flour
- 1/4 teaspoon salt
- 1 cup milk
- 2 1/2 squares unsweetened chocolate, melted
- 1 teaspoon vanilla

For Sauce Topping

- 1 egg, beaten
- 2 cups milk
- 2/3 cup sugar

Instructions

For this recipe, you will need a steamed pudding mold or baking ramekin with tight-fitting lid (one large or several small), a pot or pan for steaming, and a pre-pudding walk with the ones you love!

1. Grease pudding mold(s) and prepare steaming method.
2. Work shortening until creamy, then add sugar and continue to work until smooth.
3. Mix in beaten egg.
4. Sift flour, baking powder, and salt into mixture, alternating with milk to combine.
5. Mix in chocolate and vanilla then pour mixture into mold(s).
6. Close mold(s) and place into steam bath for 1 1/2 hours
7. For sauce, heat egg, milk, and sugar until dissolved and combined
8. Serve with sauce and whipped cream.

Bill Hackett's Notre Dame Highlight:

The '88 season was different when looking back on it. In our eyes, it was just another season where we kept on winning, week after week. It was a special season for sure. One of the things that was different was the chemistry we had that year. There seemed to be more togetherness than we had the previous year. And everyone went the extra mile, such as staying after practice to do more drills. Then there was the building momentum after beating Michigan the way we did, and then Miami. Coach Holtz kept telling us, "You don't have to be the best team in the country on Saturday; you just have to be the best team in the stadium." He had a vision and he was telling it to us week after week.

Hurrah for fun! Is the pudding done?

The tradition of the pudding will live on just like the Notre Dame spirit lives on in all of us who love the university. This recipe is an old Irish classic that's been in my family for generations. Although it probably originated in England, it has made its way through Northern Ireland and into my family's tummies. For decades, Steamed Chocolate Pudding has been a long-held Christmas and Thanksgiving tradition in the Hackett and Sylvia families.

I remember as a kid going to "The Farm" in Massachusetts for Thanksgiving, filling my belly with all the fixings, sitting around the table with all my family, finally, then taking a walk to see the barn and livestock. We climbed the fences and made barnyard animal noises while gazing at all the pigs and cows, well knowing that I would be returning to find big bowls of the pudding ready to enjoy. My grandfather would arrive back after our walk and shout "Hurrah for fun! Is the pudding done?"

Since then, my mom has mastered the recipe over the years and any question on preparation can be directed her way: barbarahackett1945@gmail.com.

Author's Note: This recipe pairs nicely with a glass of Mia Bella Moscato D'Asti, from Notre Dame alum Tom Sessi's ***Sessi Wine Company****.*

Brian Hamilton

Defensive Tackle #90

Brian Hamilton played football at the University of Notre Dame from 1990-1993. Brian's favorite recipe is Red Snapper Stew.

My wife and I love to eat fish a few times a week, so we're always looking for different recipes. Red Snapper Stew is one of my favorites! It's a tasty stew that's easy to make and has a healthy combination of fish, rice, and a few vegetables. You can always substitute your favorite fish for the Red Snapper. This dish has become a staple in the Hamilton household.

—Brian Hamilton

Red Snapper Stew

Ingredients

- 1 medium onion, sliced
- 1 tablespoon margarine
- 4 cups chicken broth
- 2 medium carrots, 1/4" slices (around 1 cup)
- 1/2 cup long grain rice (raw)
- 1 tablespoon lemon juice
- 1/2 teaspoon salt
- 1/4 teaspoon dried dill weed
- 1 teaspoon chopped fresh thyme (or 1/4 teaspoon dried thyme)
- 1/4 teaspoon pepper
- 10 ounces frozen baby Brussels sprouts
- 1 1/2 pounds red snapper, 1" pieces (or other lean fish fillets)
- 1 cup mushrooms, sliced

Instructions

For this recipe, you will need a Dutch oven. This recipe yields 4 servings. Prep time: 25 minutes. Cook time: 45 minutes.

1. In Dutch oven over medium heat, stir in margarine and onion. Cook until tender, about 5 minutes.
2. Stir in broth, carrots, rice, lemon juice, salt, dill weed, thyme, and pepper.
3. Bring to a boil then reduce heat, covering at a simmer until rice is tender, about 20 minutes.
4. Rinse Brussels sprouts under running cold water to separate; drain then add to Dutch oven.
5. Bring to boil again, then reduce heat and simmer uncovered for 5 minutes. After, stir in fish and mushrooms.
6. Simmer until fish flakes easily with fork, 5 to 8 minutes longer.
7. Serve and enjoy!

Chef James Revision (pictured)*: Omission of dill and Brussels sprouts, addition of mussels and clams (during last three minutes of cooking). For broth, 2 cups substituted as chardonnay with 2 8-ounce cans of fire roasted tomatoes, parsley, and fresh basil. Jasmine rice was used in place of long grain.*

Brian Hamilton's Notre Dame Highlight:

The moment that stands out most in my mind is the first game I played at Notre Dame Stadium. It was our home opener my freshman year. It was a night game against Michigan, the very first night game at Notre Dame, and there were a lot of rising stars on both sides of the ball. Running out onto the field with 59,000 screaming fans in the stadium was incredible. We won in a close game (28–24), and it is something I will never forget.

Ryan Harris

Offensive Tackle #68

Super Bowl champion, keynote speaker, and bestselling author, **Ryan Harris** inspires audiences across the nation by incorporating lessons learned throughout his ten-year NFL career. In 2015, Ryan became a Super Bowl champion after winning Super Bowl 50 with the Denver Broncos. He also played for the Houston Texans, Kansas City Chiefs, and Pittsburgh Steelers before retiring in 2016.

Beyond the field, Ryan continues to work to win. Whether in real estate, investing, startups, or non-profits, Ryan aims to make an impact in Denver and beyond. With these efforts, Ryan was awarded "Colorado Sportscaster of the Year" in 2020 and named to Denver Business Journal's "40 Under 40" class of 2021.

Today, you can catch Ryan as the radio analyst for Notre Dame football games, NFL radio broadcasts, as well as his weekday sports talk show in Denver on 92.5 FM, "Harris, Hastings, and Dover."

Super Bowl Chili

Ingredients

- 1 pound ground beef, 85% lean
- 2 red peppers, diced
- 1 green pepper, diced
- 1/2 white onion, diced
- 3 cans black beans
- 1 can garbanzo beans
- 2 cans diced tomatoes
- 2 Anaheim peppers
- 2 habanero peppers
- 2 packets chili mix
- garlic, to taste

Instructions

For this recipe, you will need a large saucepan or pot.

1. In pot, heat drizzle of olive oil, then brown the ground beef.
2. Once fully browned, add diced peppers, onions, and Anaheim peppers.
3. Cook to sweat then stir in beans, tomatoes, and garlic to taste.
4. Simmer on low heat for 90 minutes, stirring occasionally. (For additional spice, halve the habanero peppers and place the 4 chunks into the chili, 30 minutes into simmer.)

Ryan Harris off the field:

Ryan believes that together we can change the world. He believes: "It is your right to be extraordinary"; that when we embrace that right, we create positive change in the world; and that through our commitment to educate ourselves, invest in our communities, and act on our passions, real change happens. Ryan is also a published author. Check out his book, ***Mindset for Mastery****.*

Reggie Ho

Kicker #2

Reggie Ho was a kicker on the University of Notre Dame football team and played on the 1988 National Championship team. Ho went on to medical school at the University of Pennsylvania in Philadelphia, post-graduation, and is currently a cardiologist at Thomas Jefferson University Hospital. Reggie Ho's favorite recipe is his mom's Oxtail Beef Stew recipe.

Mom's Oxtail Beef Stew

Ingredients

- 4–5 pounds oxtail or mix with stew beef
- 2 cans tomato sauce
- 1 can tomato soup
- 3 beef or chicken bouillon cubes or 2–3 cans of chicken broth
- slice of ginger
- carrots
- potatoes
- celery
- green bell pepper, chopped (only for use with oxtails and tripe, not beef)
- round cabbage (optional)
- honeycomb tripe (optional)
- 1–2 tablespoons sugar

Instructions

1. If using oxtails, parboil first for 25 minutes.
2. Heat the oil, add slice of ginger, and brown the ginger. Next, brown oxtails (or beef) then bell pepper.
3. Add water to cover contents and mix in bouillon or chicken broth, tomato sauce, and tomato soup. Bring to a boil then simmer 1 ½–2 hours, or until meats are tender. (Oxtails may take longer.)
4. Add carrots and celery, cook for 20 minutes. Next, add potatoes and cabbage, cook another 20 minutes. Then, add sugar and season with salt.
5. If adding tripe:
   a) Clean tripe and parboil with a couple of cloves of garlic for about 15 minutes.
   b) Cut into pieces and add to pot when adding carrots.
6. Best to eat the following day.
7. Skim off fat and thicken with cornstarch as needed.

Reggie Ho's Notre Dame Highlight:

I think the Michigan game (September 10, 1988) would be my best memory. It was the first home game of my senior year, the first time I ever got to start. I had a feeling I was going to start because I was on the first team. The night before, Coach Stewart confirmed my hunch. When I ran out onto the field, knowing that I was Notre Dame's starting kicker, that truly was my most memorable moment at ND. Another huge highlight for me was kicking an extra point against Navy the year before. That was my first play in a game. I could have died and gone to heaven at that point. Even if I never made another play at Notre Dame, I would've been totally okay with that. It was amazing to have any part in Notre Dame football!

This is my mom's Oxtail Beef Stew recipe. It's always been my favorite dish growing up in Hawaii. Back in the 70s, we would often go to my parent's beach house in Laie, a small town on the north shore of Oahu, where Manti Te'o, Robby Toma, and Kona Schwencke grew up. One day, my Aunt Jeanne brought over some oxtail stew with tripe. It was a big hit! My mom added her own personal touch and it's been a favorite of mine ever since. I have very fond memories of our beach house (fishing with my dad, spearing tako and spiny lobsters, and crabbing in the evening), always anticipating a big bowl of rice with oxtail stew and a touch of shoyu at the end of the day. My mom still makes it for me when I visit Hawaii. It brings back wonderful memories of my family and childhood growing up in Hawaii every time.

—Reggie Ho

Lou Holtz

Head Coach

Coach Lou Holtz has always been a huge supporter of mine, and I'm thrilled to be able to include his favorite Pumpkin Cake recipe in my *Domer Dishes* cookbook. Kris Conner, his executive assistant, submitted this recipe on his behalf.

—Lisa Kelly, Author

Pumpkin Cake

Ingredients

For Cake

- 2 cups sugar
- 2 teaspoons baking powder
- 2 teaspoons cinnamon
- 2 teaspoons baking soda
- ½ teaspoon salt
- 2 cups flour
- 3 eggs
- 2 cups pumpkin
- 1 cup oil

For Icing

- 1 stick butter, softened
- 8 ounces cream cheese
- 1 teaspoon vanilla extract
- 1 box powdered sugar

Instructions

For this recipe, you will need a cake pan and two mixing bowls. Preheat oven to 350 degrees.

1. Combine and mix all cake ingredients.
2. Grease and flour baking pan.
3. Add mixture and bake 30-40 minutes.
4. Meanwhile, combine and mix all icing ingredients.
5. Once cake has cooled, frost and serve.

Coach has left such a long and lasting impact on not only his players, but upon so many of us. I find myself using his "Holtz-isms" almost daily, and I think my kids can recite them even before I say them. I'm sure you know many of them as well, such as: **"Trust, Love, Commitment"**; Coach's rules, **"I follow three rules: Do the right thing, do the best you can, and always show people you care"**; and of course, **"For those who know Notre Dame, no explanation's necessary. For those who don't, no explanation will suffice."** Please enjoy his favorite Pumpkin Cake recipe!

Clint Johnson

Wide Receiver #8

Clint Johnson played football at the University of Notre Dame from 1990-1994 and has had a diverse post-football career, which includes practicing law and coaching high school football. Clint currently is the director of development for the Athletes for CARE foundation. Clint's favorite dish is his mom's Pepper Chicken Fettuccine Toss.

My mom made this for me as a light meal packed with carbs and protein. I used to eat it almost weekly in high school during football season. Still love it today and make it for my kids!

Pepper Chicken Fettuccine Toss

Ingredients

- 1 1-pound package fettuccine, uncooked
- 1/4 cup olive or vegetable oil
- 3 whole boneless, skinless chicken breasts (about 18 ounces)
- 2 cups fresh mushrooms, sliced
- 2 large red peppers
- 2 large yellow peppers
- 1 medium green pepper
- 1 medium onion
- 1 teaspoon any salt-free herb seasoning
- 2 tablespoons Parmesan cheese, grated

Instructions

For this recipe, you will need a pasta pot and a large skillet.

1. Prepare fettuccine as package directs; drain when done.
2. Cut all peppers and chicken into strips, dice onion, and slice mushrooms.
3. Over medium heat, warm oil in skillet then add chicken, peppers, onion, mushrooms, and seasonings.
4. Cook and stir until chicken is cooked through, 8 to 10 minutes.
5. Add cooked fettuccine and Parmesan cheese to pan, toss to coat.
6. Serve immediately, refrigerate leftovers.

Clint Johnson's Notre Dame Highlight:

My favorite memory on the field was when we played Stanford my senior year. Playing against Head Coach Bill Walsh on the road was a really big deal for me; having a 106-yard kickoff return that day was huge. I was named the ABC player of the game. The next week, I made it into Sports Illustrated. That's the biggest highlight of my playing days at Notre Dame, hands down. Student-wise, graduation day was my favorite off-the-field Notre Dame memory.

Realizing that I was receiving my degree from the University of Notre Dame was an amazing feeling. You didn't really get acknowledged at graduation; they didn't call out your names individually, but rather by each school. But the fact that I had met all the requirements, graduated, and was heading out into the world… that was an incredible day. Another favorite memory is the first home game of my freshman year against Michigan in 1990. Coming out of the tunnel for the first time, under the lights, out into that packed stadium was truly unforgettable.

Author's Note: This recipe pairs nicely with a glass of Sessi Napa Valley Chardonnay, from Notre Dame alum Tom Sessi's ***Sessi Wine Company****.*

Lisa Kelly

Author & Alum

This is my favorite breakfast casserole that I like to make on holidays when I have lots of people over to the house. The prep work is all done the night before. All you have to do is pop it in the oven in the morning and it's ready in an hour. It's a fan favorite in my household that always has them coming back for seconds (and oftentimes thirds). I hope you love it as much as we do!

Overnight Blueberry French Toast

Ingredients

For Casserole

- 1 large loaf French bread (about 8 cups, day old is best)
- 8 eggs
- 2 ½ cups half & half (or other milk)
- ⅓ cup sugar
- 2 teaspoons cinnamon
- 2 teaspoons vanilla extract
- ½ teaspoon salt
- 1 cup fresh blueberries (or frozen blueberries tossed in 1 tablespoon flour to keep from bleeding)
- 1 8-ounce package cream cheese, light or regular
- ¼ cup raw sugar (optional, for sprinkling on top)

For Blueberry Sauce

- 1 cup water
- ½ cup sugar
- 2 tablespoons cornstarch
- 2 cups blueberries

Instructions

For this recipe, you will need a 9″x13″ casserole dish, a large bowl, and a small saucepan.

1. Grease casserole dish with butter.
2. Cut French bread into 2-inch cubes and set aside.
3. Cut cream cheese into cubes. For easier cutting, put in freezer for 15 minutes.

4. In large bowl, combine eggs, half and half, sugar, cinnamon, vanilla, and salt. Whisk until completely mixed.
5. Put one half of bread cubes into dish.
6. Top with half of cream cheese cubes and half cup of blueberries.
7. Add remaining bread cubes and top with remaining cream cheese and additional half cup of blueberries.
8. Pour egg mixture over bread cubes. (Make sure bread is completely soaked by egg mixture.)
9. Cover with plastic wrap and store in refrigerator for at least 2 hours and up to 48 hours.
10. Once chilled, preheat oven to 375 degrees.
11. Remove plastic wrap and sprinkle casserole with raw sugar.
12. Cover casserole with foil and bake 30 minutes.
13. Remove foil and bake an additional 20–30 minutes or until center is firm and bread is slightly brown on top. Set aside to cool.
14. In a small saucepan combine sugar, water, and cornstarch until simmering.
15. Add blueberries and simmer for 10 minutes. Using a fork or whisk, slightly break up the blueberries to desired consistency.
16. Cool sauce slightly before serving. Keeps in refrigerator up to 3 days.
17. Once casserole and sauce have cooled, serve. (Optional: sprinkle top with raw sugar.)

Author's Note: This recipe pairs nicely with a glass of Mia Bella Prosecco, from Notre Dame alum Tom Sessi's ***Sessi Wine Company****.*

Randy Kinder

Running Back #25

Randy Kinder played football for the University of Notre Dame from 1993-1996. He played in the NFL with both the Philadelphia Eagles and the Green Bay Packers during the 1997 season. In recognition of his special teams play that year, he was named to The Sporting News All Rookie Team (1997). He currently resides in Washington, DC, with his wife and child. He is president of the AFL-CIO Investment Trust Corporation and the vice president/ board member of the Holtz's Heroes Foundation. Randy's favorite recipe is a steak prepared in a mouth-watering marinade.

This will be the best thing you've ever tasted! Cheers!

—Randy Kinder

"Ruin a Good Steak" Marinade

Ingredients

- 4 rib eye steaks
- 1/2 cup Worcestershire sauce
- 1/2 cup soy sauce
- 2 tablespoons ground ginger
- 4 teaspoons minced garlic
- 1 teaspoon balsamic vinegar
- salt, pepper & Cajun seasoning to taste

Instructions

For this recipe, you will use a grill and need gallon-sized resealable plastic bags.

1. Combine Worcestershire sauce, soy sauce, ginger, garlic, and balsamic vinegar in gallon plastic bag.
2. Add steaks to bag and refrigerate 30–60 minutes.
3. Take steaks out and let rest for 20 minutes to an hour before cooking.
4. Coat both sides of steaks in salt, pepper, and Cajun seasoning.
5. Grill for 13-14 minutes (depending on thickness of steak) until desired temperature (I prefer mine medium rare).
6. Let rest before slicing and serving.

Author's Note: This recipe pairs nicely with a glass of Cabernet Sauvignon Howell Mountain, from Notre Dame alum Rick Mirer's ***Mirror Napa Valley*** *(see page 114).*

Randy Kinder's Notre Dame Highlight:

As far as on-the-field memories go, the win over Florida State my freshman year was amazing. To go into that game as an underdog and come out on top was a great feeling for us. For me personally, the comeback over Purdue late in my junior year was a huge accomplishment. I scored the winning touchdown in the final minutes of the game (Randy's 52-yard touchdown run stalled a strong Purdue rally in the 1995 35-28 thriller).

There are some guys who remember every single detail of every play. I am the kind of guy that, when the play turns on, my memory turns off. But during that Purdue comeback, I remember that Purdue had just scored the tying touchdown on a turnover; and when we got the ball back, I remember Ron Powlus coming into the huddle and telling us, "We've got to get this game back. Let's do this right now." On the next play we ran, I scored the winning touchdown and we took the game back.

Louis Manello

Football Student Manager & Head Lacrosse Manager

Louis Manello was a Notre Dame football student manager for three years and went on to become the head student manager for the lacrosse team his senior year. He graduated in 1986 and lived in Europe for twelve years, which is where he met his wife, who is from Belgium. This is one of the first meals that she made for him when they were dating, as he wanted to try something "typically Belgian." This is also one of the first meals they cooked together. They still cook this as their go-to meal for family celebrations. Cheers!

Carbonnade Flamande (Belgian Beef Stew)

Ingredients

- 3 pounds chuck roast
- 2 onions
- 3 tablespoons butter
- 24 ounces of very good brown beer (Belgian beers like Chimay bleue or Leffe brune are best, but you can substitute any dark beer.)
- 2 tablespoons brown sugar
- 2 laurel leaves
- 1 teaspoon dried thyme
- 2 slices of bread
- 2 tablespoons good mustard
- salt and pepper

Instructions

For this recipe, you will need a Dutch oven or large pot.

1. Trim the beef of excess fat and cut the meat into large cubes. Season with salt and pepper then peel and dice the onions.
2. Melt butter in Dutch oven or pot and brown the meat on all sides in small batches. This step is very important as it adds flavor to the meat and sauce.
3. Once browned, put meat aside and cook onions on low heat for about five minutes or until they are translucent.
4. Turn the heat up and add beer. Use a wooden spoon or spatula to scrape up the browned bits and pieces, as this will also add flavor.
5. Return meat to pot and add brown sugar, laurel leaves, and thyme.

Instructions (cont.)

6. Spread the mustard on bread slices and place the bread on top of the meat. Close the lid, lower the heat, and cook for two and a half hours.
7. When time is up, stir the meat and sauce, and taste. Cook for another 10 minutes uncovered to slightly thicken the sauce.
8. In Belgium, we always serve this dish with Belgian fries (French fries were actually first created in Belgium). However, mashed potatoes or tagliatelle would work as well.
9. Note that this dish is even better the next day so it can be prepared ahead of time and reheated before serving.

CAM McDANIEL

RUNNING BACK #33

CAM McDANIEL played running back at the University of Notre Dame from 2011 to 2014 and hails from Coppell, Texas. You may remember the photo snapped of him in the Notre Dame–USC game, October 19, 2013, which went viral, captioned: "Ridiculously Photogenic Football Player." Today, Cam and his wife, Stephani, live in Fort Worth, Texas with their three children. They are board members of The Justice Reform and founders of Purity & Majesty,

a company that utilizes micro-enterprise to restore and empower survivors of human trafficking by connecting them to the voice of God and the body of Christ in their city. Cam's favorite dish is his Golden Dome Brisket!

Golden Dome Brisket

Ingredients

- 12–14 pound brisket
  (with thick slab of fat on one side)

For Dry Rub

- 2 tablespoons coarse salt
- 2 tablespoons chili powder
- 2 teaspoons freshly ground black pepper
- 2 teaspoons ground cumin
- 4 teaspoons sugar

For Smoking

- mesquite wood chips
- apple juice

Instructions

For this recipe, you will use a smoker and need two pans, foil, and butcher paper.

1. Rinse brisket then mix together dry rub ingredients.
2. Evenly coat brisket in dry rub, wrap, and set in refrigerator overnight.
3. When ready, preheat smoker to 240 degrees. Add wood chips and fill one pan with apple juice to provide moisture.
4. Place brisket in shallow pan inside smoker for 9 hours or until thickest part reaches 165 degrees.
5. After 9 hours, wrap brisket tightly in foil or butcher paper then return to smoker, reducing heat to 225 degrees, cooking until internal brisket temperature reaches 200 degrees (ensure thermometer reads the meat, not fat).

Instructions (cont.)

6. Rest your brisket. DO. NOT. SKIP. THIS. STEP. Resting allows those hot and bubbly juices to settle down and redistribute to the meat. It also brings your brisket to the perfect temperature to slice and serve (the brisket can increase 5–10 degrees during rest period).

Discussion & Tips

Wrapping the brisket is one of the most crucial steps, in my opinion, to achieving a super juicy, tender brisket with that killer dark, caramelized bark. The brisket gets wrapped like a present, folding edge over edge until sealed, and placed back into the smoker, folded edges down.

I wish I could tell you an exact time that smoking will take, but alas, that's kind of the beauty of BBQ. It's done when it is done. For the initial smoke phase, I plan about 8 hours at 225 degrees for my 12–13 pound briskets to reach 165 degrees. However, your brisket will enter a phase in between 145 and 165 degrees where the liquid evaporating from the surface of the brisket will cool it while your grill is trying to cook it. This is called the stall, and the time frame is different during this phase for every brisket I've ever cooked. This is where a good internal thermometer comes in.

The second phase (once it's wrapped in foil or butcher paper), can take anywhere from 5 to 8 hours. I usually plan an extra 2 hours for each of my brisket cooks because if it is done early, I can always set it in a cooler and serve hours later. I don't think the brisket drops even 1 degree over 6 hours wrapped in a cooler.

Bottom line: plan for anywhere from 12 to 18 hours to fully cook your brisket (this includes the initial smoke to 165 degrees and the wrapped smoke to get your meat up to 202 degrees Fahrenheit).

Devon McDonald

Linebacker #45

Devon McDonald played football at the University of Notre Dame from 1988-1992 and was drafted in the fourth round of the National Football League Draft by the Indianapolis Colts. He played three years with the Colts, two years with the Tampa Bay Storm, and has spent his post-football career serving others. Devon currently is the Pro NFL associate director at Cru—Athletes in Action, which strives to help athletes, coaches, and their wives become devoted followers of Jesus Christ for their whole lives so that together they can be positive influencers everywhere they go. Devon's favorite recipe is Jamaican Curry Chicken.

Jamaican Curry Chicken

Ingredients

- 1/4 cup curry powder, divided
- 2 tablespoons garlic powder
- 1 tablespoon seasoned salt
- 1 tablespoon onion powder
- 2 teaspoons salt
- 1 sprig fresh thyme, leaves stripped
- 1 pinch ground allspice, to taste
- 2 1/4 pounds whole chicken, cut into pieces
- 3 tablespoons vegetable oil
- 3 cups water
- 1 potato, diced
- 1/2 cup chopped carrots
- 2 scallions (green onions), chopped
- 1 1"-piece fresh ginger root, minced
- 1 Scotch bonnet chile pepper, chopped, or to taste

Instructions

For this recipe, you will need a large bowl and a large skillet, as well as salt and pepper to taste. Recipe serves 6.

1. Whisk garlic powder, seasoned salt, onion powder, thyme leaves, allspice, salt, pepper, and half the curry powder together in a bowl. Add chicken and evenly coat with mixture.
2. Heat oil and remaining curry powder in skillet over high heat, until curry powder changes color, 2–3 minutes. Add chicken to the hot oil mixture and reduce heat to medium. Add water, potato, carrots, scallions, ginger, and chile pepper to skillet.
3. Cover skillet and simmer until chicken is cooked and gravy is thickened, 30 to 40 minutes. Leave chicken to cook undisturbed for last 15 minutes and ensure the thickest part of the thigh, near the bone reads at least 165 degrees. Remove chicken and place in serving dish, simmering gravy, uncovered, to thicken if needed. Serve chicken with gravy.

Devon McDonald's Notre Dame Highlight:

My most memorable, shining moment came on the field in 1991. It was my biggest game at Notre Dame against Michigan (I think in 1991) when I had eighteen tackles against the Wolverines. I hated Michigan. I hated those helmets—those are some ugly helmets. My last game at ND was pretty great as well. I was the defensive MVP at the Cotton Bowl on January 1, 1993 vs. Texas A&M.

Cook's Notes

The key to curried chicken is allowing the curry to cook properly. Make sure your curry has had enough time to cook!

Also try a meatless version with veggies in the place of chicken!

I usually use just over half of the scotch bonnet pepper, but some peppers are hotter than others.

This Jamaican curry chicken recipe can be served with rice or rice and peas/red beans. I like it with either—it is delicious. This was one of my mother's best dishes. It seems like she made it better each time. I thought Jamaicans invented curry until a few years ago I read that curry is native to India. Jamaica has been influenced by the native Indian culture. I hope you enjoy it. This dish is traditionally served on white rice or in a roti, but feel free to get creative!

–Devon McDonald

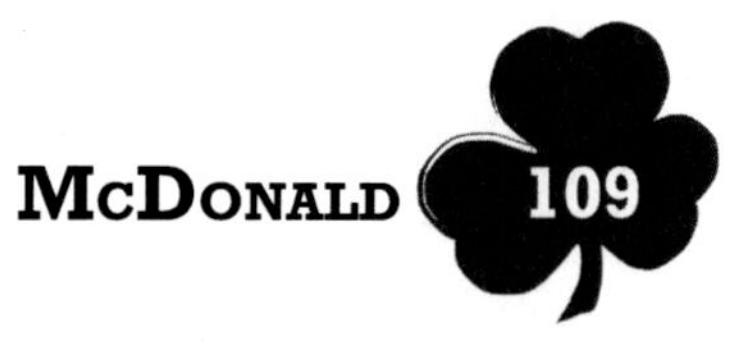

Justin Meko

Defensive Back #32

Justin Meko played football at the University of Notre Dame, graduating in 1999. He was subsequently drafted by a more formidable force than any NFL team, the US Army. As a Transportation Corps officer, he served as a platoon leader, a company executive officer, and the battalion adjutant. When his military commitment ended in 2003, he leveraged his logistics experience to secure a job with the Norfolk Southern Corporation. Today, he works for Amtrak as the Vice President of Operational Safety.

Here is Justin's wife's Cornbread Stuffing... *Best enjoyed after a Thanksgiving weekend victory over USC!*

Chrissy's Goal Line Defense Cornbread Stuffing

Ingredients

- 1 batch of cornbread, crumbled (about 8 cups, made in advance)
- 1 tablespoon olive oil
- 1 pound Italian sausage
- 9 tablespoons butter, divided
- 1 large onion, chopped
- 2 celery ribs, chopped
- 4 garlic cloves, minced
- 1 teaspoon fennel seeds
- 2 teaspoons dried thyme
- 2 teaspoons sage
- 1 ½ cups pecans, chopped
- 1 large Granny Smith apple, peeled & chopped
- ½ cup dry, white wine
- 1 cup low sodium chicken broth
- 2 tablespoons fresh parsley
- ½ cup Parmesan cheese

Instructions

For this recipe, you will need a baking sheet, a skillet, a 9"x13" baking dish, as well as salt, pepper, and olive oil to taste. Preheat oven to 300 degrees.

1. Place crumbled cornbread on large baking sheet. Bake at 300 degrees until slightly dried (about 20 minutes). Meanwhile, add olive oil to skillet over medium heat.
2. Add sausage to skillet and brown, breaking apart with spoon (about 15 minutes) then remove with slotted spoon and drain on a plate.
3. Remove grease from pan and return to medium heat, adding 6 tablespoons of butter, onions, celery and season with salt and pepper.
4. Sauté until softened (about 10 minutes) while scraping browned bits from bottom of pan. Then add garlic, fennel, thyme, sage, apples, and pecans, sautéing until apples are tender (about 5 minutes).

Instructions (cont.)

5. Preheat oven to 350 and lightly grease baking dish. In a large bowl, mix cornbread, sausage, cooked vegetables, cheese, and parsley. Taste for seasoning and add more salt, pepper, and herbs as desired.
6. Deglaze the pan over high heat with wine and broth. Add liquid to cornbread mixture and stir well. If dry, add more broth. Transfer mixture to baking dish and dot with remaining butter.
7. Cover with foil and bake until hot (about 60 minutes). Then, remove foil and bake until lightly browned on top (about 15 minutes). Serve immediately or cover with the foil and keep warm until needed.
8. ENJOY!!! Leftovers taste just as great as the initial dish and I promise... you'll be stuffed!

Justin Meko's Notre Dame Highlight:

Well, I have a couple of them! Beating Tom Brady and Drew Brees during my senior year at Notre Dame is a lot more special now than I realized at the time. My son likes to tell his friends that his dad beat Tom Brady, and he's not lying. Coach Holtz's last game at Notre Dame Stadium was a special memory since he's on the Mount Rushmore of Notre Dame coaches. That day, I went from crying at the Miami loss in 1985 to crying over Coach Holtz, the man who had turned the program around, leaving Notre Dame.

The off-season workouts were not fun, but they were memorable—they brought the team together and were brutal from a physical standpoint; you had to push each other to survive. Trekking across campus in freezing temperatures at 6 A.M. on January mornings for grueling workouts quickly bonded those experiencing it. It was invigorating to see the band of brothers rallying around each other as we all struggled to find the energy to endure. Another special memory was my first play in Notre Dame Stadium; my parents were there, and it was awesome to share the culmination of a childhood dream with the two people who supported and encouraged it most.

Rick Mirer

Quarterback #3

Rick Mirer played quarterback on the University of Notre Dame football team from 1989-1992. Rick was the second overall pick in the 1993 NFL Draft, selected by the Seattle Seahawks. He played for twelve seasons for seven teams: the Seahawks, Bears, Packers, Jets, 49ers, Raiders, and Lions. Currently, he resides in Southern California and owns a winery in Napa Valley: Mirror Wines. Rick's favorite recipe is his baby back ribs.

I've got some serious meat-eaters in my house. This rib recipe pleases all of them. We finally got it right. Also, the ribs pair perfectly with Mirror Cabernet Sauvignon!

Rick's Best Baby Back Ribs

Ingredients

- 1 rack of pork baby back ribs (2–3 racks for 3–4 people)
- BBQ sauce of choice

For Dry Rub

CAN USE SPICES OF CHOICE, JUST DON'T FORGET THE BROWN SUGAR!

- 4 tablespoons brown sugar
- 1 tablespoon kosher salt (or omnivore salt)
- ground black pepper, to taste
- 1 tablespoon garlic powder
- 1/2 tablespoon onion powder
- 1 tablespoon dried oregano
- 1/2 tablespoon of cayenne pepper (or less, unless you like it hot)
- 1/2 tablespoon chili powder

Instructions

For this recipe, you will need foil and a baking sheet. Also, you will finish on a grill. Preheat oven to 250 degrees.

1. Mix dry rub spices then apply over ribs.
2. Wrap ribs in foil and place on baking sheet.
3. Cook at 250 degrees for 2 1/2 to 3 hours.
4. When done, coat ribs with BBQ sauce and grill for 20 minutes.

Rick Mirer's Notre Dame Highlight:

I have so many great memories. Some of the simple things are what make up some of my best memories: the camaraderie, the travel, spending Thanksgiving together. My all-time best football memory, however, has to be the 1992 Penn State game. There was so much drama at the end of that game...going for two points to win the game, playing our last game in Notre Dame Stadium. We ended our time at Notre Dame on a huge highlight. The one we got to sleep on was the Penn State game, and we could not have asked for a better ending (final score: Notre Dame 17–Penn State 16). After the Michigan game ending in a tie and being left with such a weird feeling after that game, I just felt that we had to go for it. We're either going to win this thing or not.

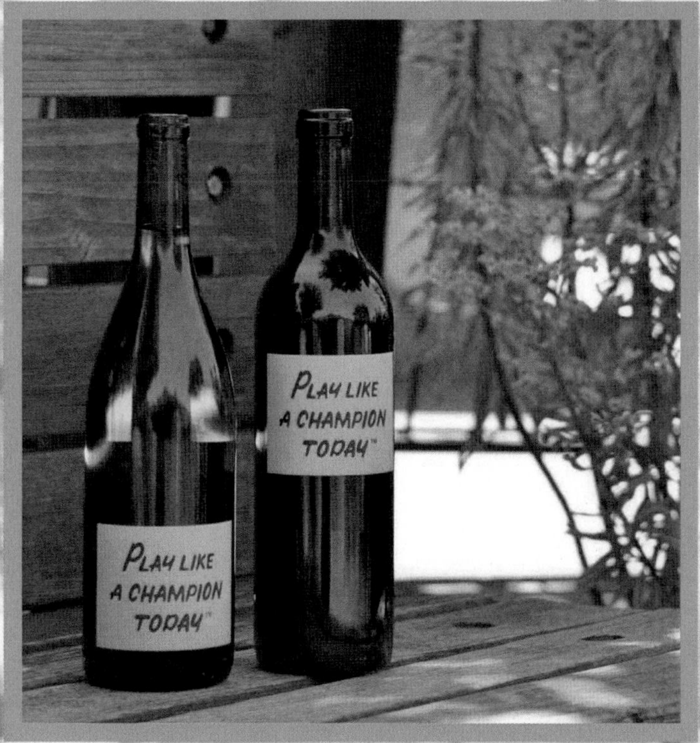
PLAY LIKE
A CHAMPION
TODAY™
PLAY LIKE
A CHAMPION
TODAY™

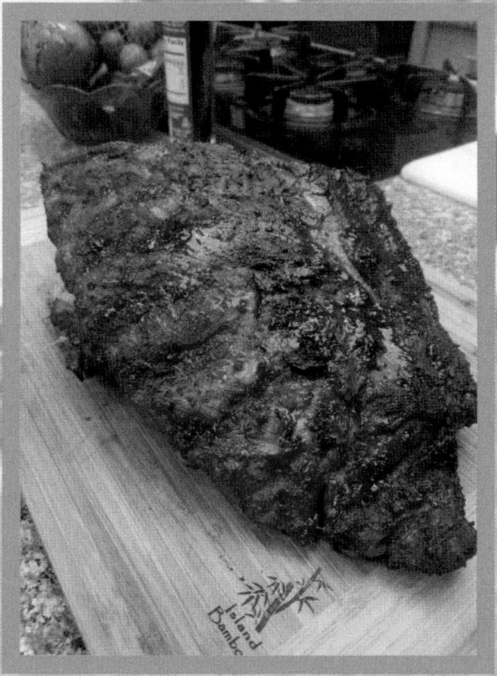

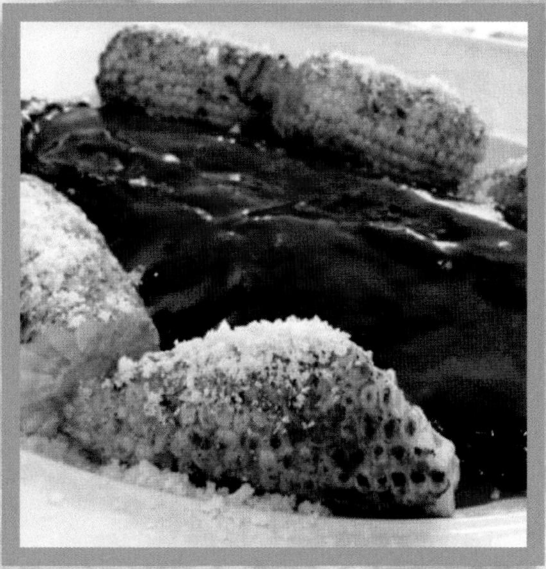

Raki Nelson

Wide Receiver #9

Raki Nelson played wide receiver at the University of Notre Dame and graduated in 2002. Today, Raki works with his three brothers in their family business, Dirty Dog Hauling: Junk and Trash Removal. They are big in the mid-state area (Pennsylvania) and offer franchise opportunities to entrepreneurs who want to provide professional junk-removal services in their area (www.dirtydoghauling.com). Raki's favorite recipe is Chicken Pot Pie.

Chicken & Dumpling Pot Pie

Ingredients

- 5 chicken legs (with thighs)
- 8 medium potatoes
- 2 quarts chicken broth
- 2 cups all-purpose flour
- $1/2$ tablespoon baking powder
- 2 tablespoons butter
- 2 cups whole milk
- 2 tablespoons olive oil
- salt and pepper
- corn starch (to thicken gravy)

Instructions

For this recipe, you will need a large pot, a large bowl, and a rolling pin.

1. Peel and cube the potatoes. Then, add chicken, potatoes, and broth to large pot. Bring to a boil then reduce to a low, soft boil until chicken is fully cooked, approximately 40 minutes.
2. While chicken is cooking, combine flour, olive oil, baking powder, butter, and 1 cup of milk together. Mix into a dough.
3. Place dough on the counter and use rolling pin to flatten, making some flat dumplings and some ball-shaped dumplings.
4. When chicken is fully cooked, remove from heat and debone. Add chicken back to pot and add the remaining milk, then bring the mixture back to a boil.
5. Use corn starch as needed to thicken the mixture and drop flat and ball-shaped dumplings into the pot.
6. Cook for a few minutes until dumplings are done and enjoy!

Raki Nelson's Notre Dame Highlight:

The LSU game my junior year at Notre Dame has to be one of the most memorable games during my time at ND. We beat them on their own turf the year before, this

time in South Bend under the lights. Mark Roman was the lights-out free safety for the Tigers, but we had a lot of wide receivers who were hungry to play football. Our offense had been opening up all day long. I only had one pass in the first half and had to wait for the fourth quarter before I saw more action. I had three catches in the final drive, ending with a catch that I took into the end zone, followed by a huge hit. Somehow, I was able to hold onto the ball and that was the game winner. That was such an awesome experience for me, a huge win under those Notre Dame Stadium lights.

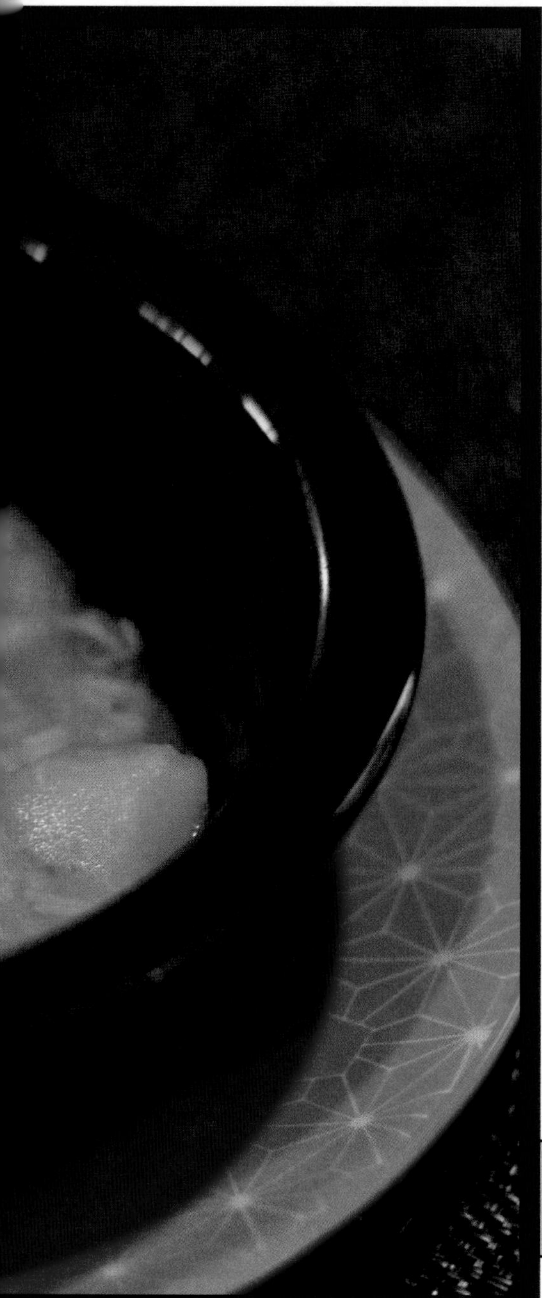

I remember that moment as if it happened yesterday: the perfect pass from Jarious Jackson, the catch. . . boom. . . touchdown! Celebrating in the end zone with Autry Denson as he lifted me up in celebration. Incredible. My second favorite memory: the first time I was introduced as a starter at a pep rally. Hearing the hype song and the roar of the crowd. Those were the moments you lived for.

Tim O'Neill

Running Back #35

Tim O'Neill played football at the University of Notre Dame from 1999-2002. He currently is a managing director at Sequent Energy and lives in Houston, Texas with his wife and children. He is also a published author of the book, ***Every Play Every Day: My Life as a Notre Dame Walk-On***. Tim's favorite recipe is his Pretzel Chicken recipe.

This recipe makes me and the whole family happy.

PRETZEL CHICKEN

INGREDIENTS

- 4 boneless skinless chicken breasts
- pretzel sticks (Rold Gold)
- 1/4 cup Greek yogurt
- 2 tablespoons Dijon mustard
- olive oil

INSTRUCTIONS

For this recipe, you will need a large pan and use an oven.

1. Cut chicken breasts in two, lengthwise. So, if there's a full breast, you would end up with 4 pieces with each side of the breast cut in two.
2. Take pretzel sticks (this is key, must be Rold Gold) and blend them in a food processor or put them in zip top bag and smash. Don't make them into crumbs, leave some chunks.
3. Tenderize breasts, either with a meat tenderizer or other method. Then, mix together Greek yogurt and Dijon mustard.
4. Brush mustard and yogurt mixture all over chicken then roll/pat down chicken breasts one at a time into smashed pretzels. Try and get as much pretzel on the chicken as possible.
5. Preheat oven to 350 degrees. Meanwhile, sauté each breast on both sides in olive oil for a few minutes on each side to brown.
6. Finish in oven at 350 degrees for 15 to 20 minutes.

While I was at Notre Dame, I started writing a journal to document my experiences as a walk-on for Notre Dame. When I started writing (during my sophomore year), it was more of a diary, a reflection at the end of each day. During my fifth year, I wrote a lot more. Finally, a few years after graduation, I got around to compiling the entries into a book and publishing my story. I didn't write it to make money; I wrote it because I truly believe in its message: to not underestimate yourself, your dreams, and what you're capable of doing.

—Tim O'Neill

Tim O'Neill's Notre Dame Highlight:

I had five amazing years at Notre Dame, and I have absolutely no regrets. I can look back and honestly say that I wouldn't have done anything differently and that I gave 100 percent. I worked harder as a Notre Dame football player than I had ever worked in my life, both physically and mentally. The experience was full of ups and downs, successes and failures, along with the inevitable disappointments when you thought you were going to get playing time and didn't. But in the end, it was absolutely worth it.

Frank Pinn

Running Back #34

Frank Pinn played football at Notre Dame and graduated with a marketing degree. He currently resides in the Chicago area with wife Liz Pinn (Majewski '89) and children Mary, Frank, and John. Frank's favorite recipe is Chicken and Sausage Cacciatore.

I've enjoyed cooking from a young age, primarily because I loved eating. Another reason is the fond memories I had in the kitchen with my Grandma Betty. I shared my favorite recipe with friends and roommates at ND. Now, I enjoy cooking with my family. This is a perfect fall dish that can be prepared for Notre Dame football Saturdays. Growing up in Chicago, we added our own spin on this classic dish: the Italian sausage really amps up the flavor. Cacciatore, also called Hunter's Stew, honors the harvest of nature to develop strong, warm, hearty flavors, with love. Great thing about this recipe is it can be made in one pot which holds all day as the game goes on! Have fun with this dish—you can free-hand the portions or ingredients based on desired tastes.

Chicken & Sausage Cacciatore

Ingredients

- 8 bone-in skinless chicken thighs (or boneless thighs and add chicken breast)
- 12 ounces Italian sausage (3 links), cut into 2″ chunks
- 1 medium white onion, diced
- 3 bell peppers (1 each green, red, yellow), diced
- 1 large carrot, peeled and diced
- 16 ounces mushrooms (variety recommended: Cremini, White Button, Porcini)
- 3 Roma tomatoes, quartered
- 4 sprigs fresh thyme, destemmed
- 4 sprigs fresh rosemary, whole
- 2 fresh sage leaves, finely diced
- 2 tablespoons Italian parsley, roughly chopped
- 6 cloves garlic, minced
- 2 teaspoons Herbs of Provence
- 12 ounces crushed tomatoes
- 2 tablespoons tomato paste
- 1 ½ cups white wine (or red to preference)
- ½ cup chicken broth
- olive oil, salt, and pepper to taste
- Parmesan, grated

Instructions

For this recipe, you will need a Dutch oven pot and a large insulated bowl or warmer.

1. Generously season the chicken with salt and pepper.
2. Heat drizzle of olive oil in Dutch oven pot, sear chicken on both sides until golden brown, about 10 minutes. In same pot, sauté Italian sausage with chicken 10 minutes, then remove meat from pot and place in large bowl or warmer (to be added later).
3. Add another drizzle of olive oil to same pot, sauté onion and carrot then add remaining veggies (garlic, peppers, mushrooms, Roma tomatoes and fresh herbs). Cook until softened, then add tomato paste and herbs of Provence. Sauté another 5–10 minutes.
4. Add wine to deglaze, scraping pot to mix in fond (browned bits) from caramelized veggies. Cook to reduce, about 3 minutes. Add crushed tomatoes and chicken broth. Stir; add more salt, pepper, or other spices to taste.
5. Replace chicken and sausage with juices back to pot, stir to marry flavors.
6. Preheat oven to 350 degrees if using baking method. Cover pot and braise down 40–50 minutes. Remove lid and bake 5–10 minutes or simmer on stove 1 hour.
7. Serve with pasta, polenta, or roasted potatoes along with crusty bread to mop up the savory sauce.

Photos by Frank Pinn

Frank Pinn's Notre Dame Highlight:

Since my dad played football at Notre Dame, having my family come join me on the field after a game is among my fondest memories. Another unforgettable memory is being in Sports Illustrated (April 1986). That photo is more than a bunch of guys at football practice—it represents how Coach Holtz made everything into a competition. The reason why we (Mike Gatti, Brad Alge, & I) were in that photo is because we were first to sprint over and hear Coach's end-of-practice talk. You did not just walk or jog over, you ran. It was a prize to be front row when he started talking. As the last competition of every practice, I did my best to be in the front—I wanted to show I cared. On that particular day Sports Illustrated was there to capture the moment. I was in my dorm getting ready for practice when one of my high school buddies called me. He blurted out, "You're in Sports Illustrated!" I told him to stop messing around so I could get to practice. I didn't believe him. When I got to practice, everyone was staring at me saying, "How'd you get in Sports Illustrated?" and I soon realized it was true!

TONY RICE

QUARTERBACK #9

TONY RICE played quarterback at the University of Notre Dame from 1985-1989 and was a member of the 1988 National Championship team. Tony Rice had never been much of a cook—that is, until the pandemic shutdown and quarantine hit. His friends (and fellow Notre Dame teammates) decided it was time to help him out. Chris Zorich, Pat Terrell, and their friend, Chef Rick DeLeon, set up weekly zoom calls where they taught Tony how to cook. This is the very first dish that Tony learned how to make.

Chicken Parmesan

Ingredients

- 2 chicken breasts, halved lengthwise to make 4 strips
- 3/4 cup Italian seasoned breadcrumbs
- 1/4 cup Parmesan cheese, grated
- 1/4 cup olive oil
- 1 cup shredded mozzarella or Italian blend cheese
- 2 cups of favorite tomato sauce
- cooking spray
- 6 ounces uncooked spaghetti

Instructions

For this recipe, you will need a large baking sheet and pasta pot, and use an oven.

1. Preheat oven to 450 degrees. Grease baking sheet lightly with cooking spray.
2. Combine breadcrumbs and Parmesan cheese in a bowl. Lightly brush olive oil onto the chicken, then dip into breadcrumb mixture to fully coat. Place on baking sheet and repeat with the remaining chicken.
3. Top chicken lightly with cooking spray and bake 25 minutes.
4. Meanwhile, place pasta in salted boiling water and cook per box instruction. Heat up sauce.
5. Remove baked chicken from oven, spoon 1/4 cup sauce over each piece of chicken and top each with 1/4 cup of shredded cheese.
6. Bake 5 more minutes or until cheese is melted.
7. Serve pasta with warm sauce on top and enjoy!

Tony Rice's Notre Dame Highlight:

Winning a national championship was, of course, a great Notre Dame moment for Tony, but playing the service academies was his most memorable experience.

Those guys (Air Force and Navy) never gave up. They went full speed ahead at you. Meeting those extremely well-disciplined teams are great memories for me. Again, they never gave up. Everyone talks about the Miami game, but beating the academies was quite an accomplishment. On any given day, they could beat you. Oftentimes, you were up for the Miami and USC games, but maybe you took the academies for granted because you outweighed them and were faster than them. That was when you'd get beat.

Ryan Ritter

Football Student Manager and head Golf Manager

Ryan Ritter, class of 2007, was a Notre Dame football student manager starting his sophomore year, working Charlie Weis's first football season, later managing golf his senior year. Ryan currently lives in Lewisville, Texas with his wife, Stephanie, and their two sons, Reid and Hudson.

I have a shirt from the ND Texas Club entitled "Top 10 Reasons Texans Go to Notre Dame." Number six is one of my favorites: "To spread the word that the ***Texas Chili at SDH just ain't how it's done at home****." Truer words have never been written! I spend more time than I should on social media preaching the Texas Chili Gospel, which includes two important commandments:*

1. Thou shalt not use beans.

2.Thou shalt not use tomatoes.

Down here, "chili" really comes from "chile," as in chile peppers. The Bowl of Red is the true Texas-trail classic. Simple ingredients that folks working a trail would easily have on hand to make a hearty meal.

Call it a "meat sauce" or "meat soup" if it makes you feel any better. I'm not morally opposed to anyone tricking up their chili with beans or tomatoes, but like the shirt says, that just ain't how it's done.

Texas Bowl of Red

Ingredients

- 4 slices bacon (the thicker, the better)
- 3 pounds beef chuck (or lean brisket), cut into 1-inch cubes
- 3 cloves garlic, minced
- 1 large white onion, diced
- 1 cup ground chile pods (I recommend guajillo and ancho as your base, adding in serranos and jalapenos if you like more kick)
- 1 tablespoon ground cumin
- 1 tablespoon salt
- water to cover beef
- Optional: 2–3 tablespoons masa harina (or cornstarch)
- Garnish: cilantro, sour cream, cheese, crackers

Instructions

For this recipe, you will need a blender or spice grinder and a large Dutch oven pot or stockpot.

1. Grind your chile pods until fine. Leave seeds in for more spice.
2. Cook four slices of bacon in pot
3. Remove bacon, mince, and place to the side. Leave all drippings in the pot.
4. Lower heat, add onion and garlic to the pot, cooking until onions are soft. Be careful not to leave the heat too high which will burn the garlic!

Instructions (cont.)

5. Increase heat to medium-high. Add beef to the pot and cook in the bacon drippings until very well browned.
6. Add in chile pod mixture, cumin, and salt. Stir contents in pot until beef is well coated in seasoning.
7. Add water to the pot, ensuring that the beef is completely covered.
8. Return bacon to the pot.
9. Once chili reaches a low boil, reduce heat and simmer for 3 to 4 hours, stirring frequently.
10. If a thicker chili is desired, make a slurry with the masa and add to chili. Start at 2 tablespoons masa in slurry, increasing by one tablespoon at a time until chili reaches desired thickness.
11. Ladle into a bowl and garnish with cilantro, sour cream, shredded cheese, and crushed crackers if desired.

JOHNNY ROMANO

LEPRECHAUN MASCOT

JOHNNY ROMANO was the leprechaun at the University of Notre Dame from 2012-2014 and graduated with a degree in marketing. Romano, who hails from Glencoe, Illinois, always wanted to be a football player, but at five-feet six-and-three-fourths-inches tall, that wasn't in the cards. So he chose the next best thing—Notre Dame leprechaun! Johnny is also a Notre Dame legacy. He is a third generation Domer, and his grandfather, Buddy Romano, was a former Notre Dame football player and a member of the 1946, 1947, and 1949 national championship squads, also known as "Leahy's Lads." Johnny and his grandfather had a very special bond, and his grandfather loved that Johnny was the Notre Dame leprechaun. Johnny currently lives in Chicago, where he is a senior enterprise account executive in tech sales. Johnny's favorite recipe is his dad's rigatoni.

Romano's Rockne Rigatoni

Ingredients

- 2 28-ounce cans crushed tomatoes
- 1 6-ounce can tomato paste
- 2 pounds hot Italian sausage
- 1 large onion, diced
- 4 cloves garlic, pressed
- 1/4 cup olive oil
- 1/2 cup white wine
- 3 tablespoons fennel seeds (whole or cracked)
- 1 tablespoon oregano
- 2 sticks butter
- 1 cup heavy whipping cream
- 1 cup Romano cheese
- 1 cup fresh parsley, chopped

Instructions

1. Heat oil and sauté onions, garlic, fennel, and oregano until onions are cooked. Add Italian sausage (without casing) and sauté while constantly stirring to break sausage into small crumbles.
2. Once sausage is cooked, deglaze pan with white wine. Add tomato paste and sauté until incorporated. Add the 2 cans of crushed tomatoes and cook for about 10 minutes while constantly stirring.
3. Add butter, cream, and Romano Cheese and stir. Cook for 10 more minutes. Be careful not to let sauce burn by stirring it constantly. Stir in fresh parsley. Use about 3 cups of sauce for every pound of pasta...rigatoni is preferred.

Romano

Marv Russell

Linebacker #54

Marv Russell played football at the University of Notre Dame on the 1973 National Championship team under Head Coach Ara Parseghian and Head Coach Dan Devine. Marv's career since graduation has been diverse, wearing the hats of author, keynote speaker, global leadership expert, and ordained Methodist minister. Note form Marv's wife, Catherine:

This is Marvin's favorite recipe that his mom made. She typically made it for family special events and parties. Even as an adult home for holidays, Marvin was notorious for cutting small slices and wrapping them in foil, then hiding them so he could continue to enjoy the egg pie later. Eventually, she learned to hide it from him, but he always found her hiding spots. She'd end up serving a pie with a big wedge missing. Grandma Russell finally shared her family recipes about twenty years ago, and I've been making egg pie for Marvin ever since. Personally, I like it for breakfast!

Mimi's Egg Custard Pie

Ingredients

For Filling

- 1 1/2 cups sugar
- 2 tablespoons flour
- 3/4 stick butter
- 4 egg yolks
- 1 1/2 cups evaporated milk or light cream
- 1 1/2 teaspoons vanilla
- prepared pie shell

For Meringue

- 4 egg whites
- 1/2 cup sugar
- 1/2 teaspoon lemon extract (optional)

Instructions

For this recipe, you will need a glass bowl, frozen beforehand, a mixing bowl, and will use an oven.

1. Preheat oven to 400 degrees. Combine sugar and flour in mixing bowl.
2. Add butter and thoroughly mix, then add egg yolks and blend well. Repeat with milk/cream and vanilla.
3. Once thoroughly mixed, pour into prepared pie shell and bake 20 minutes.
4. Reduce oven to 350 degrees and cook until pie is firm. (You can test by sticking a knife in the center.)
5. While filling bakes, mix meringue ingredients in frozen bowl and beat on high until stiff peaks. (Author's note: if you have trouble getting your meringue to fluff, add another egg white and that should do the trick!)
6. Have meringue prepared to put on hot pie as it comes out of the oven.
7. Bake at 350 degrees until light brown.

Marv Russell's Notre Dame Highlight:

You never forget the first moment when you run out of the tunnel as a Notre Dame football player. It is quite remarkable. The first home game my freshman year, running out of the tunnel on that beautiful fall day was incredible. I remember being choked up with tears in my eyes. It was pure. When

you go from the concrete and your spikes hit that grass cushion, that is why you go to Notre Dame. A Saturday afternoon doing battle on that field is one of the most perfect places in the world. You think about all of the students who have gone to ND or will go in the future—when you think about all of the people in this country who love college and professional football, you suddenly realize how blessed you are and that very few will have that experience.

Jeremy Sample

Linebacker #36

Jeremy Sample played linebacker at the University of Notre Dame from 1991-1995. Jeremy, the "Harlem Stuntman," currently resides in New York City where he works as a stunt performer/stunt coordinator in the film and television industry. Jeremy's favorite recipe is Hoppin' John. Enjoy!

Hoppin' John

Ingredients

- ½ pound dry black-eyed peas in water
- ½ cup onion, chopped
- ½ cup green bell peppers, diced
- ⅓ cup celery, diced
- 1 clove garlic, minced
- 2 tablespoons olive oil
- ½ cup long-grain white rice
- 1 cup cooked ham, cubed
- ½ pound ground beef
- 2 strips bacon
- ½ teaspoon salt
- ½ teaspoon oregano
- ½ teaspoon pepper
- ½ teaspoon red chili flakes
- 1 small bay leaf

Instructions

For this recipe, you will need a Dutch oven or oven-proof pot.

1. Rinse peas, boil for 5 minutes, cover and set aside for 1 to 3 hours.
2. Drain and rinse peas. Preheat oven to 375 degrees.
3. Sauté onions, bell peppers, garlic and celery.
4. Add ham, ground beef and bacon, and let cook with the bay leaf.
5. Add soaked peas, rice and 1 ½ cups water. Bring to boil.
6. Transfer the mixture to a 2-quart oven-proof dish.
7. Cover and bake 30 minutes, or until peas and rice are tender.
8. Remove bay leaf before serving.

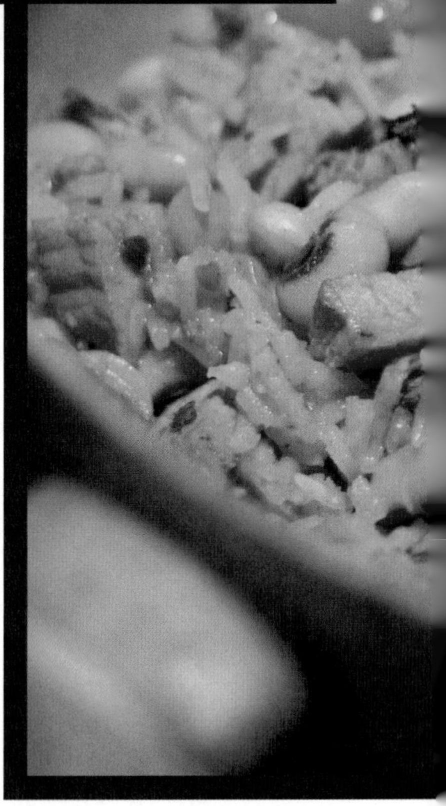

Jeremy Sample's Notre Dame Highlight:

My favorite on-the-field memory would have to be the weekend we beat Florida State. That game trumps them all. It was an incredibly exciting game, at home and at night. Battling for the number one spot in the country, we walked away with a victory. All of the focus was on us and the game. We beat a highly ranked, amazing Florida State team at Notre Dame Stadium. It doesn't get any bigger than that.

Evan Sharpley

Quarterback #13

Evan Sharpley played football (quarterback) and baseball (1B/DH/OF) at the University of Notre Dame. He was drafted in the 2009 MLB Draft by the Seattle Mariners and played for the Arizona League Mariners, the Everett AquaSox, the Traverse City Beach Bums, and the Lake Erie Crushers. He currently resides in Elkhart, Indiana, where he runs Sharpley Training.

Here you go. This is the recipe we use here at the Sharpley house for Chicken & Waffles. As far as the story, not sure I have a great one other than what's not to like about fried chicken, a ton of Irish grass-fed butter, and bourbon syrup! Breakfast Like a Champion Today!

Fried Chicken & Waffles

Ingredients

For Chicken

- 8 boneless, skin-on chicken thighs
- vegetable oil, for frying
- 2 cups buttermilk
- 2 ½ cups all-purpose flour, more if needed
- 1 tablespoon seasoned salt, Lawry's suggested
- 1 teaspoon paprika
- 1 teaspoon freshly ground black pepper
- 1 teaspoon ground dried thyme
- ½ teaspoon cayenne, or more to taste
- ¼ cup milk, more if needed

For Waffles

- 2 cups all-purpose flour
- ¼ cup sugar
- 1 tablespoon baking powder
- ½ teaspoon kosher salt
- 1 ½ cups milk
- 1 tablespoon vanilla extract
- 4 large egg whites
- 2 large egg yolks
- 8 tablespoons (1 stick) salted IRISH butter, melted

For Sauce

- 1 cup pancake syrup (your choice)
- ¼ cup bourbon (your choice)
- 4 tablespoons (½ stick) salted IRISH butter

Instructions

For Chicken

1. Thoroughly rinse the chicken, then cover all the pieces with 1 3/4 cups buttermilk. Soak in the refrigerator overnight or up to 24 hours. When ready to fry, let bowl sit at room temperature for 30 minutes to reduce chill.
2. Meanwhile, preheat oven to 360 degrees and prepare breading: add flour, seasoned salt, paprika, pepper, thyme, and cayenne in large bowl and stir together well.
3. In a small bowl, combine milk and remaining 1/4 cup buttermilk. Add to flour mixture and mix until lumps form throughout (this will adhere to chicken and make for crispier breading). If necessary, add more flour or milk to make it slightly lumpy.
4. Heat 1 1/2–2 inches of vegetable oil in a deep pan over medium-high heat until a deep-fry thermometer registers and keeps at 365 degrees.
5. Working in batches, thoroughly coat each chicken piece in breading, pressing extra onto the chicken if necessary. Place the breaded pieces on a plate.
6. Add breaded chicken to oil 3 or 4 pieces at a time. Ensure they don't stick together, then cover the skillet and fry for 5 to 7 minutes, checking occasionally to make sure the chicken isn't getting too brown. Turn the pieces over, cover again and cook 3 to 5 minutes more. Monitor the oil temperature throughout this process to prevent burning. When done, transfer fried chicken to a baking sheet (they will not be completely cooked through) and repeat steps to fry remaining chicken.
7. Bake fried chicken for 15 minutes to finish the cooking process, internal temperature at least 165 degrees at the thickest part. Cover and keep warm.

For Waffles

1. Preheat the waffle iron to the regular setting. Use KODIAK CAKE BUTTERMILK MIX or the recipe provided in the following steps.
2. In a separate bowl, whisk milk, vanilla, and egg yolks. Pour into dry ingredients and very gently stir until halfway combined. Pour in the melted butter mixing very gently until combined.
3. In a separate bowl (or using a mixer), beat the 4 egg whites with a whisk until stiff. Slowly fold them into the batter, stopping short of mixing them all the way through.
4. Scoop the batter into your waffle iron in batches and cook according to the manufacturer's directions (lean toward being a little deep golden and crisp!). Keep warm.

The Finish

1. Pour the pancake syrup and bourbon into a small pot and bring to a boil. Turn down the heat and simmer for 3 to 4 minutes. Turn off the heat and whisk in the butter 1 tablespoon at a time.
2. To serve: Place 2 chicken thighs on top of a waffle. MORE IRISH BUTTER!! Pour the warm sauce over everything and serve immediately.
3. Drink Recommendation: Sharpley Old Fashioned

   Journeyman Small Batch Cask Strength Featherbone Bourbon (120 Proof)
   + Traverse City Cherry Whiskey (90 Proof)
   + Traditional Bitters
4. Cigar Recommendation:

   My Father The Judge

ROD SMITH

CORNERBACK #21

ROD SMITH played cornerback for the University of Notre Dame football team from 1988-1991 and was drafted in the second round of the 1992 NFL Draft. He played for four NFL teams, including the Patriots, Panthers, Vikings, and Packers. Rod currently lives in Charlotte, North Carolina, and is the owner-operator at Magnolia Installers, LLC, Business Development at Magnolia Cabinetry and director at Speedway Children's Charities.

Rod's favorite recipe is Keto Friendly Almond Butter Bites.

Keto Friendly Almond Butter Bites

Ingredients

- 2 tablespoons real butter
- 2/3 cup all-natural almond butter (preferably sugar free)
- 1 cup unsweetened all-natural shredded coconut
- 4 drops of organic, sugar free vanilla extract
- 2 tablespoons Monk fruit natural sweetener
- 1 tablespoon organics cacao powder
- 1 tablespoon coarse Himalayan salt

Instructions

For this recipe, you will need a large mixing bowl and a sheet pan. Recipe yields 18 bites.

1. Soften butter in microwave.
2. In large bowl, combine the almond butter, softened butter, and cocoa powder.
3. Add Monk fruit sweetener with shredded coconut, mix well with spatula.
4. With a melon baller, scoop 2" spoonfuls onto a sheet pan lined with parchment paper.
5. Immediately place sheet pan into freezer for 15 minutes.
6. Store refrigerated in food container. As bites are sticky, keep separated with parchment paper.

My lady and I have been grinding over a keto low-carb/low-sugar healthy chocolate snack for months. We finally decided to make our own. Be warned: We are both salty over sweet fans,

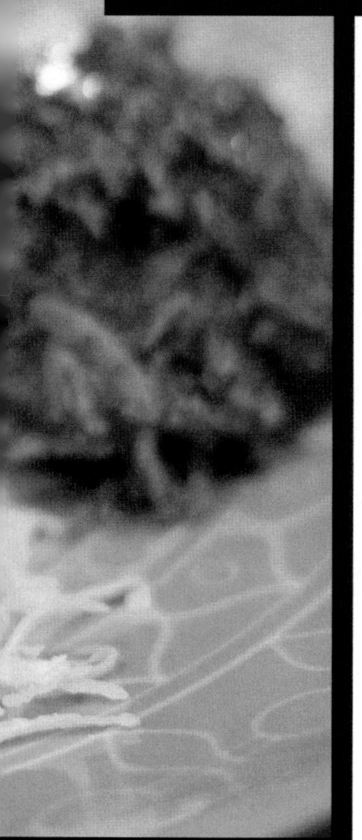

so understand that the salty crunch of the coarse Himalayan sea salt is heaven to us! Eat as many as you want, you'll stay in ketosis.

ABBs are fiber-dense and quickly satiate the most ravenous appetite. Hope you enjoy! Thank you for including us. GO IRISH!

—Rod Smith

Toryan Smith

Linebacker #49

Toryan Smith played linebacker at the University of Notre Dame from 2006-2009. He currently resides in the Miami-Fort Lauderdale area where he works in sales, helping businesses accelerate performance, productivity, and profitability through technology. Toryan's favorite recipe is Keto Chicken Tacos.

Keto Chicken Tacos

Ingredients

- 1 pound boneless skinless chicken breasts or thighs
- 2 tablespoons olive oil
- 1 avocado, diced
- 1 tomato, diced
- 1/4 cup onion, diced
- 2 cloves garlic, minced
- 2 tablespoons taco seasoning
- sour cream (optional)
- green or red peppers (optional)
- 8 leaves romaine lettuce, rinsed & dried

Instructions

For this recipe, you will need a large pan. Yields 4 servings.

1. Add chicken, garlic, olive oil, and spices in a large bowl or zip-seal bag. Allow to marinate in the refrigerator at least 15-30 minutes or up to 24 hours.
2. Remove chicken from marinade and place chicken on the grill or pan on medium heat.
3. Let chicken cook until it is no longer pink inside (165 degrees), about 9-10 minutes per side. I personally like to let the chicken cool and then chop it up to my preferred bite size.
4. Next, heat 1 tablespoon oil to cook diced peppers and onions until translucent. At this point, I add my preferred seasonings and chicken, now chopped, into the pan and stir to increase the flavoring.
5. Assembly: Layer lettuce wraps with chicken, tomatoes, avocado, and sour cream. Add your favorite taco sauce.

Toryan Smith's Notre Dame Highlight:

My best Notre Dame football memory was playing Michigan State in East Lansing my freshman year (2006), when I was just getting used to playing football, managing the hectic schedule, and balancing football and classwork. We came from twenty-one points behind to beat MSU. That's when I really felt the magic of Notre Dame. It was a big-time game and we had a quarterback competing for the Heisman. Simply put, it was an epic game, an instant classic. That game really solidified to me that I was an integral part of a big-time football program.

This is one of my favorite recipes because it provides me with an amazing tasting and nutritious meal—whether it be a snack, lunch, or dinner. I've always searched for ways to eat more healthfully, especially in the daytime because I like to have a FEAST at the end of the day for dinner! But I have always felt like I had to sacrifice the taste of my food to accomplish healthy eating. This meal is both nutritious and delicious! It also provides many options to mix and match ingredients like meats, spices, etc. For all the calorie counters, people who like to avoid carbs, and even people who just want to have a really quick and easy, tasty meal, I highly recommend Keto Chicken Tacos!

—Toryan Smith

Jack Snow

Wide Receiver #85

Jack Snow played football at the University of Notre Dame from 1962-1964. He was drafted in the first round (8th overall pick) of the 1965 NFL Draft by the Minnesota Vikings but was soon after traded to the Los Angeles Rams where he spent the duration of his career (1965-1975). Following his NFL career, Jack went into the real estate business with his college roommate Bob Arboit.

Then he returned to the Rams as a receivers coach in 1982. In 1992, he joined the Los Angeles sports-talk radio station, KMPC, as an analyst for the Rams radio broadcasts and a daily program host. He later followed the team to St. Louis when they moved in 1995. In November of 2005, Jack developed a staph infection and passed at the age of sixty-two as a result of complications.

Clam Dip

Ingredients

- 24 ounces sour cream
- 2 tablespoons lemon juice
- 1 teaspoon celery seed
- 1 teaspoon celery salt
- 1 tablespoon garlic salt
- 2 tablespoons Worcestershire Sauce
- 1 teaspoon pepper
- 1 teaspoon salt
- 2 small cans minced clams

Instructions

For this recipe, you will mix all ingredients together in a bowl. Seal bowl and chill in refrigerator at least two hours or overnight. Serve with Ruffles chips and enjoy before it disappears!

I came to know Stephanie Snow Gebel, Jack's daughter, through our dads, as they were classmates at Notre Dame. Over the years, I have supported her in spreading the word about The Snow Foundation, which was founded by Stephanie and her brother, J.T. Snow, former six-time MLB Gold Glove recipient. Jack's granddaughter (Stephanie's daughter), Raquel Gebel was diagnosed in 2010 at the age of four with a rare form of diabetes, called "Wolfram syndrome." J.T. and Stephanie have been very active in raising awareness and funding to find a drug therapy for this devastating form of diabetes. Jack's daughter, Stephanie, ever so kindly shared with me his favorite recipe in honor of her dad's memory.

—Lisa Kelly

Jack's wife, Merry Carol, got this recipe from her mother. Merry would make this dip for Jack on all major holidays and, of course, for major sporting events. The tradition continues with Jack's grandkids. They all know a celebration is in sight when they see a big bag of Ruffles chips and 'Papa's clam dip' being made.

—Stephanie Snow Gebel

Charles Stafford

Split End/Tail Back #81

Charles Stafford played football at the University of Notre Dame from 1991-1994 and spent his post-football career in the IT industry. He is currently the VP of operations for PIER Group LLC and focuses on helping people to achieve their personal and professional goals. Charles' favorite recipe is his mother's rigatoni.

As a child, one of my fondest memories was of my mother making rigatoni for the family. No matter what time of year, it always seemed to hit the spot. As one who appreciates routine and consistency, it never let me down. As I grew older and my wife adopted the recipe, the memories continued, and the joy of this dish was handed down to my children. With one notable addition—sausage. All great meals have one thing in common: They allow you to connect to a time, an emotion, and a place when the world just seems right.

Rigatoni

Ingredients

- 1–2 jars of favorite marinara sauce
(I prefer Muir Glen, basil or oregano)
- 16 ounces rigatoni
(Or your favorite noodle; I believe you should make every dish a reflection of what you enjoy.)
- 1–2 cups mozzarella cheese, shredded
- 1 pound ground beef
(Or turkey, again, what you prefer; if you do not wish to mix meats, increase to 2 pounds.)
- 1 pound ground Italian sausage or ground chorizo
(Again, it should be whatever meat you enjoy.)
- seasoning for meat
(use your preference here, whatever you enjoy.)

Instructions

For this recipe, you will need a pan, pot, and 9″x13″ baking dish. Serves four... linemen? Or 6–8 people.

1. Preheat oven to 350 degrees. Cook and drain pasta as directed on the package (or a little al dente). Set aside for addition to the baking dish.
2. Meanwhile, in a skillet, cook first meat over medium-high heat (I recommend cooking each meat separately). Cook 5–7 minutes, stirring frequently and breaking into small pieces. Drain and set aside, then repeat with second meat choice.
3. Assembly: Grease dish with cooking spray. Add marinara sauce (first layer), followed by noodles (second) then a mix of both meats (third). Repeat layers until you reach the top of the baking dish. Add mozzarella cheese as the final top layer.
5. Bake 25–30 minutes or until casserole is at least 165 degrees in center. Garnish as desired (I prefer basil).

Charles Stafford's Notre Dame Highlight:

Charles's favorite Notre Dame memory occurred during that mystical 1993 football season.

Believe it or not, my favorite Notre Dame football memory didn't involve my playing a significant role in the results we

achieved. However, what I felt in that time is something I won't soon forget. In 1993, I lived in Grace Hall, and we had a momentous win over Florida State. The #1 sign went up on top of Grace Hall and was lit up for everyone to see. The energy on campus that next week leading up to the Notre Dame vs. Boston College game—which we won't ever talk about—was electric. We had the pep rally in front of Grace Hall, and I remember being on stage and getting to speak in front of the whole student body. The campus was on fire, if you will; it was so alive. That Florida State game in 1993, even though I didn't play a major role in the game, is something I'll never forget.

Kinnon Tatum

Linebacker #2

Kinnon Tatum played football at the University of Notre Dame from 1993-1996 and was drafted in the third round of the 1997 National Football League Draft by the Carolina Panthers. Kinnon currently resides in Raleigh, North Carolina, where he's a financial services professional and generational wealth consultant at Thrivent. Kinnon's favorite recipe is this Taiwanese-Style Chicken with Jasmine Rice, Crispy Shallot, and Cilantro.

Ingredients

- 2 boneless, skinless chicken breasts
- 1/2 cup Jasmine rice
- 1/2 pound red cabbage
- 2 tablespoons rice flour
- 1 1/2 tablespoons sugar
- 1 shallot
- 2 tablespoons soy sauce
- 1 dried chile de arbol
- fresh cilantro, to taste
- olive oil
- salt and pepper, to taste
- 2 cups water, divided

Taiwanese-Style Chicken

Instructions

Preparation

1. Wash and dry the fresh produce.
2. Peel and thinly slice the shallot.
3. Cut out and discard the cabbage core; thinly slice leaves.
4. Roughly chop the cilantro leaves and stems.
5. Cut off and discard the chile stem; halve lengthwise. (For a milder dish remove and discard the seeds.) Thoroughly wash your hands and cutting board immediately after handling the chile.

The Rice

6. In a small pot, combine the rice, a big pinch of salt, and 1 cup of water. Heat to boiling on high.
7. Once boiling, cover and reduce heat to low. Cook 12 to 14 minutes, or until the water has been absorbed and the rice is tender. Turn off the heat and fluff the cooked rice with a fork. Drizzle with olive oil and set aside in a warm place.

The Sauce

8. While the rice cooks, in a medium pan (non-stick if you have one), combine the soy sauce, sugar, ½ cup of water, and as much of the chile as you'd like, depending on how spicy you'd like the dish to be. Heat to boiling on medium-high.
9. Once boiling, reduce the heat to low and cook, stirring frequently, for 3 to 5 minutes, or until the sugar has dissolved and the liquid has reduced in volume by about half. Transfer to a large bowl; carefully remove and discard the chile. Rinse and wipe out the pan.

Instructions (cont.)

The Shallot

10. While the rice continues to cook, place the flour and shallot in a medium bowl, and season with salt and pepper. Toss to thoroughly coat.
11. In the same pan, heat 1 tablespoon of oil on medium-high until hot. Once the oil is hot enough that a piece of shallot sizzles immediately when added to the pan, add the coated shallot in a single, even layer (tapping off any excess flour before adding.)
12. Cook, stirring frequently, 2 to 4 minutes, or until browned and crispy. Transfer to a paper towel-lined plate; immediately season with salt and pepper. Wipe out the pan.

The Chicken

13. Pat the chicken dry with paper towels; season with salt and pepper on both sides. In the same pan, heat 2 teaspoons of olive oil on medium-high until hot. Add the seasoned chicken and cook 4 to 6 minutes on the first side, or until browned. Flip the chicken and add ¼ cup of water to the pan. Cook 4 to 6 minutes, or until the chicken is cooked thorough.
14. Leaving any liquid in the pan, transfer the cooked chicken to a cutting board. Using 2 forks, carefully shred into bite-sized pieces. Transfer to the bowl of sauce. Stir to coat. Set aside in a warm place.

The Cabbage & Plating

15. Add the cabbage to the pan, and season with salt and pepper. (If the pan seems dry, add ¼ cup of water.) Cook on medium-high, stirring occasionally, 5 to 6 minutes, or until wilted and the liquid has cooked off.
16. Divide the cooked rice between 2 dishes. Top with the cooked cabbage and shredded chicken. Garnish with the fried shallot and cilantro.

Kinnon Tatum's Notre Dame Highlight:

Without a doubt, my best Notre Dame football memory is the one that made me immortal—the 1995 game against USC. The notable, huge play was violent, destructive, and absolutely game-changing—that was the moment. USC came in, talking up a big game. They were making all kinds of noise about how they were going to come into our house and beat us. Yadda, yadda, yadda... Bring it on. I have slingshots in reserve! (Kinnon laughs.) Yes, they were coming to town and it was a big match-up, but we were ready. That play could not have been any bigger as far as turning points in games go.

We were actually down 7–3 at the time; and after that play, we went for thirty-five straight points. It was hands down the turning point in the game. I wish they would have shown me walking off the field. You think Johnny Cash is cool? Walking off the field, I just knew that play was going to be all over SportsCenter that night and that little red light was going to be blinking on my dorm phone when I got back home. That was my moment. I'm so glad that I played football when I did. My job was to be a "trained assassin," to "kill" people in games. Nobody was protected. Today, I would probably be ejected from every game.

Aaron Taylor

Offensive Guard #73

Aaron Taylor played football for the University of Notre Dame from 1990-1994. He was a two-time All-American, Lombardi Award-winning offensive guard, and team captain for the Irish. The Green Bay Packers chose him in the first round, sixteenth pick overall, of the 1994 National Football League draft. He is a Super Bowl XXXI champion (with the Green Bay Packers) and retired from football at age twenty-eight. Currently, Aaron is a college football analyst for CBS Sports. His mission in life is to live to serve, which includes (but isn't limited to) feeding the homeless on Christmas Day at Horton Plaza in downtown San Diego, mentoring with the AthLife Foundation, and creating The Joe Moore Foundation for Teamwork. Here is Aaron's favorite Cinnamon Raisin Baked Bliss! Please allow for a two-hour nap after eating.

Cinnamon Raisin Baked Bliss

Ingredients

- 8 eggs
- 3/4 cup milk
- 1/4 cup cinnamon vanilla Coffee-mate creamer
- 1/4 cup water
- 1/2 teaspoon cinnamon
- 1 tablespoon vanilla extract
- 1 1/2 cups brown sugar
- 3/4 cup chopped pecans
- 1 1/2 sticks butter
- 1 1/2 cups maple syrup

- 1 loaf cinnamon raisin challah bread, sliced in ¾″–1″ thick (You can get away with thinner cinnamon raisin bread, or plain challah if you absolutely must, but make no mistake, it will NOT be as good as the cinnamon raisin challah loaf.)

Preparation

For this recipe, you will use a blender and an oven. You will need foil and multiple 9″x13″ baking dishes, depending on batch size.

Instructions

1. Place eggs, milk, creamer, water, cinnamon, and vanilla into blender and mix thoroughly at low speed to avoid frothing.
2. Generously butter baking dishes and place slices of bread (cut in half, vertically, or triangles) in bottom of dishes.
3. Pour egg mixture over bread then add your preferred amount of the brown sugar to taste. If 0 was no sugar, and 10 was completely covered with sugar, I go about a 7.
4. Cover dish with foil and refrigerate overnight, or until bread soaks up excess egg mixture.
5. Preheat oven to 350 degrees and bake 50–60 minutes. Halfway through baking, remove foil and add a pat of butter to each slice of bread. Sprinkle lightly with chopped pecans and more brown sugar as preferred. Finish baking and let cool slightly before serving.

IMPORTANT

Combine the maple syrup with 1/2 stick of butter and slowly melt together approximately 5 minutes before eating. This combination alone will do wonders for even frozen Eggo waffles!

PERNELL TAYLOR

RUNNING BACK #46

Taco Soup

Pernell Taylor went from Bishop Amat Memorial High School in La Puente, California, to the University of Notre Dame where he played running back for legendary Head Coach Lou Holtz from 1985-1987. Pernell currently lives in Ontario, California, and works in law enforcement for the city of Los Angeles. Pernell's favorite recipe is his mom's Taco Soup.

This recipe was given to me from my mom and three of her sisters about twenty years ago. I make it often and hope you enjoy it as much as I do!

Ingredients

- 1 pound ground beef or turkey
- 2 cans diced tomatoes
- 2 cans kernel corn
- 2 cans beans (kidney, black, pinto)
- 1 package taco mix

Instructions

For this recipe, you will need a stock pot. Also include tortilla chips and variety of cheeses to your liking.

1. Cook ground beef or turkey and drain.
2. In stock pot combine tomatoes, corn, beans, meat, taco mix, and 2 cups of water.
3. Bring to a boil, stirring constantly to prevent sticking.
4. Let simmer for 15 minutes.
5. Ladle into bowls, adding grated cheese and tortilla chips.
6. Serve and enjoy!

COURTNEY WATSON

LINEBACKER #33

COURTNEY WATSON, who hails from Sarasota, Florida, played football at the University of Notre Dame from 2000-2003. Courtney went on to play in the NFL for the New Orleans Saints, Buffalo Bills, and Houston Texans. He's now settled back in his hometown of Sarasota. Courtney's favorite recipe is his mom's collard greens.

This recipe was passed down to my mom from her mom and grandmother. It's a favorite of mine and our family's.

Mom's Collard Greens

Ingredients

- 3–4 bags chopped collard greens
- 1 pack of turkey wings (smoked) or 1 pack of smoked neck bones
- 1 cup Zesty Robusto Italian dressing
- 1 green bell pepper
- 1 pack dry onion/mushroom soup mix (Lipton)
- 1 tablespoon real bacon bits
- 2 tablespoons sugar
- 2 tablespoons vinegar
- Mrs. Dash Table Blend, to taste
- red pepper flakes, optional
- 2 tablespoons olive oil

Instructions

1. Wash meat and put in a large pot with enough water to cover meat. Add olive oil and bring to a boil, then simmer until meat is done.
2. While meat boils, wash collards. Make sure rinse water runs clear, filling collards container with water and pouring out. Once water is no longer green and runs clear, drain collards and slowly add to cooked meat.
3. Cook collards with meat on medium boil. Add sugar and vinegar to cut bitterness. In a bowl, add soup mix with ½ cup water and stir. Add mixture to collards. At this point, add preferred seasonings, or my recommendation: Robusto Italian Dressing (1 cup or to your taste), Mrs. Dash, pepper flakes, chopped peppers and real bacon bits.
4. Stir occasionally to make sure collards and meat do not stick to the bottom of the pot. After all ingredients are added, simmer with top on and cook for 2–3 hours, adding seasoning throughout, to taste. Don't add any more water at this point.
5. Enjoy with jasmine rice and cornbread.

Courtney Watson's Notre Dame Highlight:

Off the top of my head, the first thing that comes to mind is when I got to speak at the pep rally before the Michigan game (it was either my fifth year or my senior year). At the time, I was on the student senate and my Zahm Hall guys were seated front and center at the pep rally. They all made signs with my headshot from the football program on them. Fifty or sixty of them chanted "Senator Watson" through the whole pep rally—no matter who was speaking, including Coach Willingham—until it was my turn to speak, of course, and then they got quiet.

On the field, my favorite memory would have to be playing (and beating) Florida State in Tallahassee. Being from Florida, I had a ton of family and friends at the game. I also had an interception. To play well enough to beat FSU on their home turf was a huge high for me and for the whole team. There were very few games that I remember being nervous before, having butterflies, and not being able to control my emotions—this was one of those games.

Brandon Wimbush

Quarterback #7

Brandon Wimbush played quarterback at the University of Notre Dame from 2015-2018 and hails from Teaneck, New Jersey. Brandon finished his college career as a graduate transfer at the University of Central Florida. He is currently a founding partner (along with Ayden Syal, Notre Dame, class of 2017) of an online agency called "MOGL," which plans to build a social network between athletes and companies looking for promotional representatives and brand ambassadors. Brandon's favorite meal is a medium sirloin steak, accompanied by mashed potatoes and mixed veggies, recipe courtesy of Chef James Ketara. Let's dig in!

Medium Sirloin
with Mashed Potatoes & Mixed Veggies

Ingredients

- 1 12-ounce top sirloin ("baseball steak")
- 3 small Yukon gold potatoes
- 3 tablespoons unsalted butter
- 2 tablespoons sour cream
- 2 tablespoons canola oil (if cooking indoors, on cast iron)
- 3 tablespoons chimichurri, recipe to follow (optional)
- salt and pepper

For Chimichurri

- 1 bunch cilantro
- 1 bunch parsley (flat leaf)
- 3 cloves garlic
- 6 tablespoons red wine vinegar
- 4 tablespoons fresh squeezed lemon juice
- 1/4 cup olive oil
- salt and pepper

Preparation

For this recipe, you will use a pot, a large (cast iron recommended) pan or grill, and optionally a food processor.

Pictured: Chef James Ketara

Chef's Note:

Mixed vegetables were not added to the picture because this tends to be a preference option. If you're grilling, though, asparagus and zucchini planks work well with this dish. Add lemon halves to the grill face down to flavor those veggies as well.

Instructions

1. On a small plate, salt and pepper steak, set aside, and bring to room temperature, approximately 25 minutes.
2. In a large saucepan or medium stock pot, bring 5 cups of salted water to a boil. Wash and dice potatoes, adding to boiling water. Cook until fork tender.
3. If grilling, get your grill smoking hot to build crust to hold in the render.
   If using cast iron, add the canola oil, and heat until smoking.
4. Cook steak 5 minutes on the first side, then flip and finish for another 3–4 minutes (depends on thickness). Remove from heat and set aside to rest.
6. Remove potatoes, strain, and add to a mixing bowl, or the bowl of a stand mixer with the paddle attachment.
7. To the potatoes, add butter, sour cream, and salt and pepper to taste. Mash or whip to combine.
8. After steak has rested 5 or so minutes, slice into medallions. Spread mashed potatoes and add the medallions atop the potatoes.
9. If using chimichurri (instructions below), use a spoon to liberally dress the medallions.

For Chimichurri

1. In a food processor, add the first 5 ingredients, and pulse until broken down.
2. Begin adding the olive oil slowly while constantly running the processor.
3. Salt and pepper to taste.

Chris Yura

Safety, Fullback, Special Teams #23

Chris Yura played football at the University of Notre Dame from 2000-2002. Chris's favorite recipe is his Grandmother Yura's pirohi recipe.

I was raised in West Virginia by my amazing parents who came from families of different cultures and backgrounds: My mother is 100% Appalachian and my dad is 100% Slovakian. Both cultures and cuisines are delicious and provided the much needed fuel for early athletic pursuits and current ambitions. For my favorite recipe, I decided to go with my Slovakian heritage because it is the first food I can remember telling others about and trying to correctly pronounce it with the accent I had heard my dad and grandmother use. As I started to spread the news of this delicious dish with my slight Appalachian accent, my pronunciation was undoubtedly incorrect. Listeners would look at me with confusion as I described this food that was so good and plentiful in my grandparents' home. Finally, as I got older, I was in the midst of this

Grandma Yura's Pirohi Recipe

detailed description when someone asked, "Are you talking about pierogis? Yeah, they have those in the freezer aisle." Now, I know many readers will have had the common pierogi, but Mrs. T's pierogis cannot compete with Grandma Yura's. So give this recipe a try and taste the difference. When these become a staple at your house, remember they are pronounced "pirohis" not "pierogis"!

Ingredients

- 4 eggs
- 1 1/2 teaspoons salt
- 1 teaspoon oil
- 3 pounds potatoes
- 6 cups flour
- 1–2 cups lukewarm water
- 3/4–1 pound sharp cheddar cheese, cubed

Instructions

Potato Filling

1. Cook potatoes and mash.
2. While hot, add cheese cubes and mix until cheese is melted.
3. Use potato filling to fill Pirohi dough squares.

Pirohi Dough Squares

4. Sift flour, salt. Add eggs, oil, and warm water to make a soft dough. Turn on lightly floured board.
5. Gently knead for 5 minutes. Allow to stand 10 minutes before rolling out dough very thin.
6. Cut into 2" squares and place 1 teaspoon filling in the center of square. Fold over dough square to form triangle or rectangle. Pinch ends tights.

Time to Cook

7. Cook in boiling water. Allow to simmer until they float on the top- about 5 minutes. Drain.
8. Pour (optional) browned butter over and serve hot.

Chris Yura's Notre Dame Highlight:

It is extremely hard to select one memory as my best Notre Dame football memory. There are so many moments that I remember. The first time I walked out of the tunnel and onto the field at Notre Dame Stadium was incredible. It was quite an accomplishment to get the opportunity to play as a true freshman, to get the chance to play in the home opener—"Kickoff Classic"—against Kansas in 1999. I got such a sense of awe seeing the fans: The spirit of the crowd, walking out of the tunnel, the feeling of being on the field for the first time, and knowing the responsibility of what I had to do. I don't think I had run faster in all my life as I did on that opening kickoff. But at the same time, I was so nervous. A few short months before, I was playing with high school kids, and then I was facing guys who had three and four years under their belts. I had been training in camp and felt prepared for the job, but nothing truly had prepared me for that moment.

MALIK ZAIRE

QUARTERBACK #9

MALIK ZAIRE played quarterback for the University of Notre Dame from 2013-2016 and finished his final year of eligibility as a graduate transfer student at the University of Florida. Malik is currently a college football TV analyst for CBS Sports and continues to give back to his beloved alma mater. Malik's favorite recipe is Banana Surprise. Let's check it out!

BANANA SURPRISE

INGREDIENTS

- 3–6 bananas, unpeeled with ends cut off
- 5–10 Medjool dates, remove pits and chop to preferred size
- 10–20 ounces applesauce (If store bought, use a jar of organic applesauce with no added sugar or additives.)
- natural sweeteners, optional (brown sugar or coconut sugar)
- spices, optional (cinnamon, nutmeg)

For this recipe, you will need a baking sheet or pan (glass or metal), knife, fork, spatula, spoon, bowl, and heat-resistant gloves or potholders. With metal sheet, line with parchment paper. Serves 2–3 people.

Instructions

1. Preheat oven to 425 degrees.
2. Place bananas (with peel on) in the baking dish.
3. Cover with a piece of parchment paper.
4. Bake bananas for 10 to 15 minutes. Then take them out to check and flip them. (Length of time depends on how ripe the bananas were to start with.) If very ripe, they will take less time to bake. Check after about 8 minutes and flip them.
5. When fully baked, remove bananas. (The peels should be mostly black and banana juice dripping from the ends.)
6. Slit each banana horizontally from top to bottom.
7. Using a spatula or knife and fork, transport your bananas one by one to your bowl(s). Open each banana up with your knife and fork and gently scrape out the baked banana meat and juice into your bowl(s). Discard the peels.
8. Add your applesauce and chopped dates.
9. Add sweetener and/or spices to taste (optional).

Chris Zorich

Defensive Tackle #50

Chris Zorich played football at the University of Notre Dame from 1987-1990. Chris began at Notre Dame as a linebacker but was moved to nose tackle early in his career. He never looked back. Chris played on the 1988 National Championship team and was drafted in the second round of the National Football League Draft by the Chicago Bears where he played from 1991-1996. He also played one year for the Washington Redskins. Chris is currently a partner at Randall Partners, LLC. Chris's favorite recipe is Ahi Poke Bowl.

AHI POKE BOWL

INGREDIENTS

- 1 large sushi-grade ahi tuna steak, finely diced
- 1/2 sweet onion, finely chopped
- 1 teaspoon fresh grated ginger
- 1/4 teaspoon red pepper flakes
- 3 tablespoons soy sauce
- 2 tablespoons sesame oil
- 1 avocado, diced
- 3/4 cup brown rice or spring mix
- non-stick coconut oil spray
- 2 teaspoons toasted sesame seeds or rice flavoring
- 1 scallion, finely chopped

PREPARATION

For this recipe, you will need to cook your rice of choice to use in plating, and an appetite for something delicious!

This is my favorite recipe, primarily because of who makes it for me...my wife! She started making it for me when we were dating, and I absolutely loved it. The night I proposed to her, it just happened to be the dish she made for me. I hope you enjoy it as much as I do!

Instructions

1. In a large bowl, stir together tuna steak, onions, ginger, red pepper flakes, soy sauce, and sesame oil.
2. For stacks:
   a) Generously coat a ¾ cup measuring cup with non-stick spray.
   b) Press ahi mixture into the bottom half of the cup, add a layer of avocado, then fill the rest of the cup with rice, pressing down firmly with a spoon to compact the mixture.
   c) Quickly turn mixture out onto serving plate. Repeat with remaining tuna, avocado, and rice.
3. Garnish salad stacks or bowl with a sprinkling of sesame seeds (or rice topping) and green onions.
4. Serve and enjoy!

TOs
PITTSBURGH
0
TOs
NOTRE DAME
0
15:52
QTR
DOWN
TO GO
BALL ON

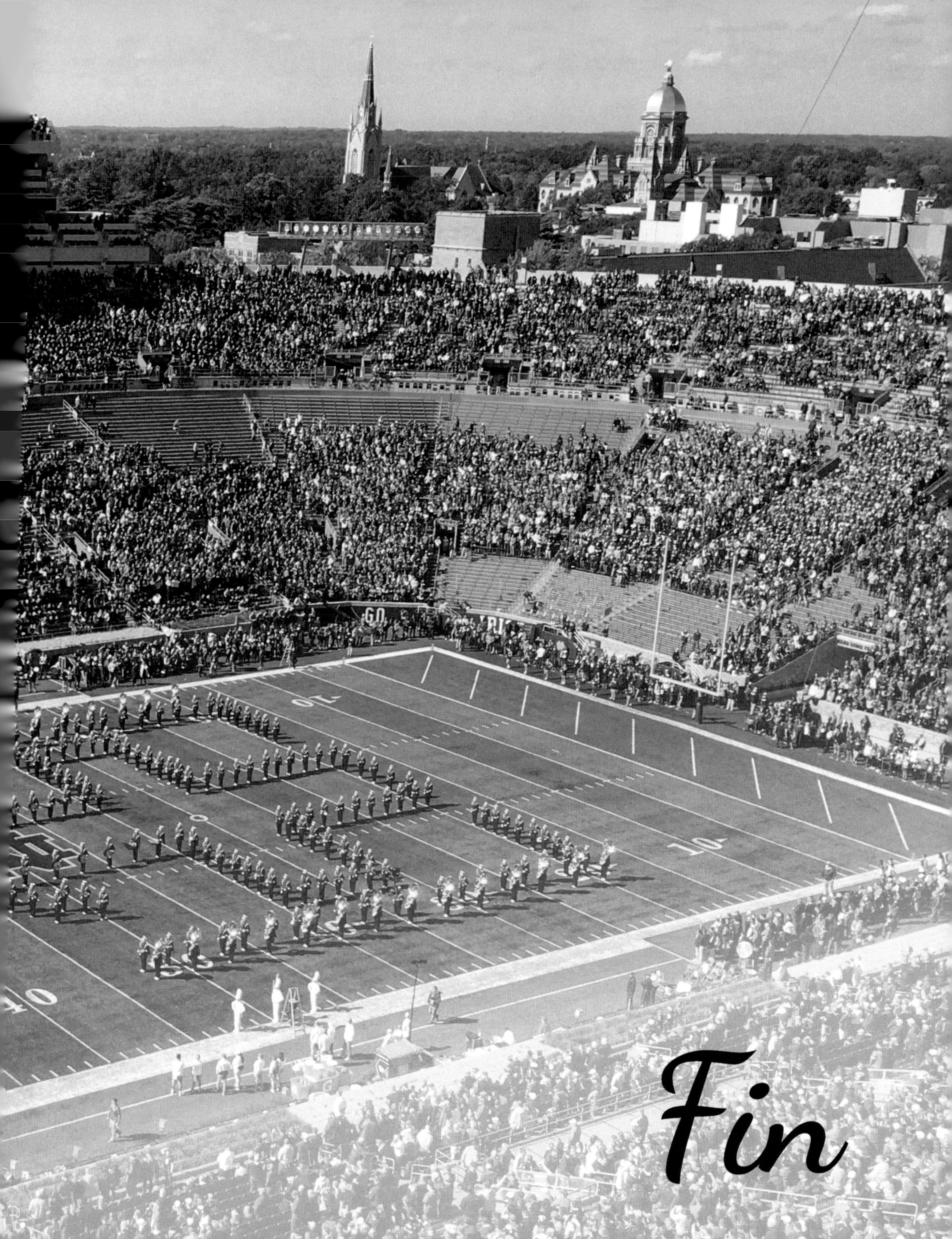
Fin

Lisa Kelly had no choice but to love Notre Dame football. Ever since she can remember, Notre Dame football has been a part of her life. She learned her first colorful word at the tender age of three during the Notre Dame–USC game on a Thanksgiving weekend spent at her grandparents' house. She and her family made annual pilgrimages to Notre Dame to spend football weekends with her dad's college roommate and his family. Notre Dame football has always been an integral part of her life.

As a Notre Dame grad herself (business major), Lisa made sure she took advantage of three things in her four years. First, becoming a student of theology at the most renowned theologian institution in the world. Second, studying English to support her passion for effective communications, no matter her career direction. Finally, and most importantly, leaving this great university with a degree in business and a specialty in marketing. Armed with these tools she engages the world, continuing to use what she so aptly calls, the "Notre Dame Value Stream."

Lisa began her professional career in the not-for-profit sector, working for the Better Business Bureau (BBB). She taught people how to be better-informed consumers and served as a dispute resolution arbitrator. She expanded her career horizons by branching further into her career field, working thirteen years as a marketing professional in Yellow Pages advertising. The fast-paced environment in an agency setting and the creative outlet energized her career.

In 2007, she took a leap from the advertising world and

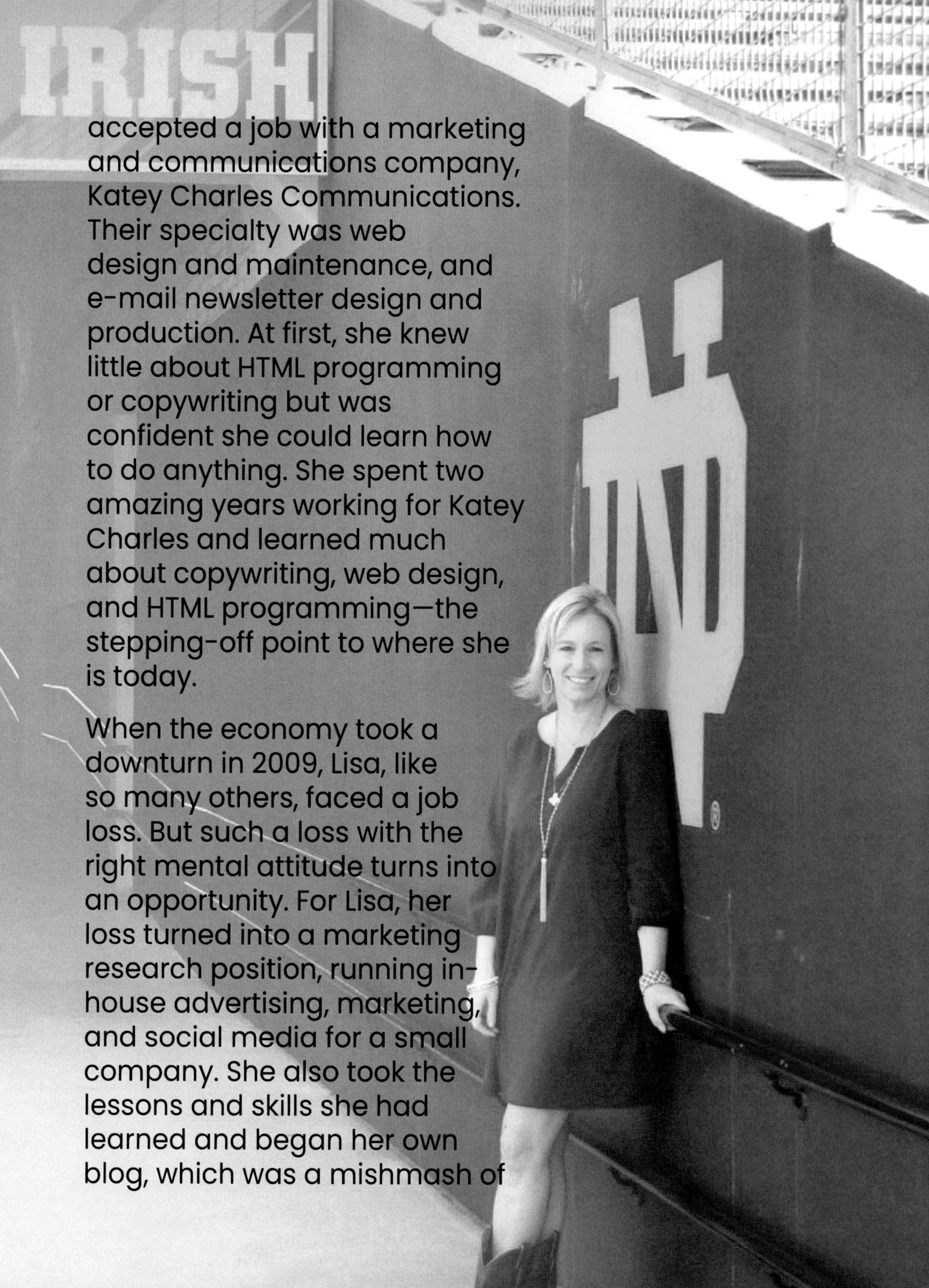

accepted a job with a marketing and communications company, Katey Charles Communications. Their specialty was web design and maintenance, and e-mail newsletter design and production. At first, she knew little about HTML programming or copywriting but was confident she could learn how to do anything. She spent two amazing years working for Katey Charles and learned much about copywriting, web design, and HTML programming—the stepping-off point to where she is today.

When the economy took a downturn in 2009, Lisa, like so many others, faced a job loss. But such a loss with the right mental attitude turns into an opportunity. For Lisa, her loss turned into a marketing research position, running in-house advertising, marketing, and social media for a small company. She also took the lessons and skills she had learned and began her own blog, which was a mishmash of digital marketing best practices, motherhood, music flashback, and sports. Blogging is hard work, taking patience and perseverance. Lisa's perseverance was the catalyst for a major life change.

In 2011, Lisa was contacted on Twitter by an advertising agency who was working on a contest sponsored by Volvo and the Big East Conference to determine the "Biggest Fan of the Big East Conference." She was selected to compete for the title of "Biggest Fan," along with fifteen other alumni writers representing the sixteen schools in the Big East Conference. As basketball is not really her forte, Lisa dug inward for this contest. After eight writing assignments, a trip to New York City for media day, a trip to her alma mater for the Notre Dame–Syracuse match-up, and endless self-promotion on social media, Lisa rose to the top and was crowned the "Biggest Fan of the Big East Conference." In all honesty, Lisa never expected to win this contest; but the more she thought about it, "losing" really is not in her vocabulary. If you're going to do something, give it your all and shoot for the top.

Shortly after the contest, Lisa realized she was constantly defending Our Lady's University. People were quick to find the shortcomings of Notre Dame and those associated with it, and Lisa really wanted to do something that would showcase all the positive things that emerge from Our Lady's University. And that is how her first book, "Echoes From the End Zone: The Men We Became," took shape. Her first interview was with former tight end Oscar McBride. It was more like two friends catching up, but it was a wonderful walk down memory lane with Oscar and a discovery of how Notre Dame helped shape him into the man he is today. Lisa realized that this was the beginning of something special. One interview led to another. As she completed each interview, it was clear that a theme was emerging. Even though Lisa and these former players all came to Notre Dame from vastly different backgrounds, they all had similar experiences and each credited their time at Notre Dame and the Notre Dame Value Stream with playing a huge role in molding them into the people they are today.

Lisa currently has three books in the "Echoes From Notre Dame" book series: *Echoes From the End Zone: The Men We Became*, published in 2013; *The Men We Became: More Echoes From the End Zone*, published in 2016; and *Triumphs From Notre Dame: Echoes of Her Loyal Sons and Daughters*, published in 2019. *Domer Dishes: Inside the Lives and Kitchens of Your Fighting Irish Gridiron Greats* is Lisa's first cookbook.

Currently, Lisa is an e-content specialist in the eCommerce Department at Nestle Purina PetCare. Over eighty interviews and four books later, Lisa is still enjoying how wonderful it is to be able to share these positive stories about Our Lady's student-athletes. In Lisa's words, "There are so many of these stories yet to be told." She hopes that you have enjoyed her journey through the lives of these loyal sons and daughters of Our Lady's University and the stories they tell. Lisa's four books only touch the surface. She looks forward to continuing the journey and sharing more remarkable stories of her loyal sons and daughters. Lisa is currently working on several projects including a Notre Dame Baseball book, not yet titled.